Evil in the Boardroom

The Perils of Venture Capital / Courage through Faith

Dewayne E. Adamson

ISBN: 1497320801
ISBN 13: 9781497320802

Table of Contents

Evil in the Board Room /

The Perils of Venture Capital / Courage Through Faith

This is a personal story of hard work and success, with one of the ventures having been destroyed by the machinations of the venture capital world. A must read for any entrepreneur seeking working capital.

A study guide on the do's and the don'ts when working with investors. Real secrets to starting a business and making it a success.

How to avoid the pitfalls, overcome adversity, and wage a comeback.

Alternative Titles:

An entrepreneur's guide to start-ups

A story of inspiration and hardship overcome

A beginner's guide to starting a business

A lesson in raising angel investment money

A study of the mechanics of venture capital

Dealing with success and failure

Coming back from adversity

Salvation and victory

Forward

My initial intent when I started this project was strictly to document the series of events in the order they occurred during the collapse of Plan Express. My son Bart and I would talk endlessly about how on earth a company that was doing so well could suddenly be destroyed by others in spite of our best efforts to successfully grow our company. As we would debate and identify actual points it became apparent to me that I would be constantly forced to relive and replay them for the rest of my life unless I wrote it down.

What I ended up with was a long summary list of actual events that then begged to be explained in further detail. I would sit on my computer at night and then add some further explanation in order to tie out one event to the next, all in an effort to ease my mind and rationalize it.

After a month or so of this sort of documentation I decided that the education I received during this part of my life needed to be shared with others who may venture down a similar path. I would not want anyone to ever have to endure the pain and stress of this story with nowhere to turn, when here were clear examples of things to avoid or tips on how to deal with some of the circumstances they may go through.

Once that decision was made I then added some personal parts of my life in order to bring a sense of reality that a reader could empathize with. As the book was originally going to be a basic business book about Angel funding and Venture Capital the text was basic and dry. As I added the personal and historical aspects it added color but not to the point of reading like a novel. I do believe you will find plenty of deception, intrigue and emotion in the book however.

It is my hope that there are clear lessons to be learned here and that this book will provide you with direction, caution and yet give you hope.

1

In the Beginning

Clearly etched in my mind as if it were yesterday is my view from the street as I walked toward kindergarten class about five blocks away. I looked back through the front window of our three-room flat in the worst section of Kenosha, Wisconsin—Fifteenth Ave. between Sixty-Third and Sixty-Fifth (ask anybody)—and saw two feet crossed at the ankles, wearing white socks, and flung over the back side of the couch. No good-byes and no warning.

That was the last time I saw my father until I was ten. It was that next time, as a ten-year-old, that he took my sister and me to see the movie *The Walking Dead* at the theater. That didn't work out so well. I had nightmares for years. As a result of that encounter, I really had no problem with not seeing him again for another nine years.. That next time was at his scheduled appearance in a courtroom as my mother tried to collect back child support.

My name back then was Ellis Adamson. It stayed that way until the first day of first grade when the teacher called out my name and the classmate next to me yelled out "his name is Alice, that's a girl's name" even at six years old, I knew right away that Ellis was going to be trouble. So quickly I became just Dewayne.

1

I hadn't started out life in Kenosha, we'd been forced to move there. I was born in Lake Geneva where we lived in a small house that was near my Fathers brother and it was in a nice neighborhood. My father was working as a mechanic but he decided he wanted to buy a gas station so he asked my grandfather for a loan. Wanting to support his daughter and grandson, my grandfather loaned my father the money. However, within 2 years, my father lost it all. With not a lot of other choices, we up and moved to Kenosha, where my father took a job at the Rambler plant.

After my father left, my mother, now a single mom and the sole provider in 1959, worked at the Kenosha Theater selling tickets for twenty-five cents a seat. Then she scored a job selling Kirby vacuums. This wasn't the best of situations as it was usually night work and she weighed all of 90 lbs and had to carry these gargantuan vacuum cleaners and all the accessories. I cannot imagine her lugging all this up stairs.

Being quite young, I don't remember a whole lot more about that time, although I do remember mom being very stressed. Within a couple of years, she married a giant of a man named Miles, whom I was afraid of. The good thing about that was that he had a job in the parts department at the Ford dealership, so we were able to move to a nice house, which we lived in for the next four years.

Miles drank a lot. Maybe this had something to do with his accident with a train. That's right, a train! I don't know exactly what happened but I do remember seeing his bloody clothes in a brown paper bag. I think he was in a coma for a while and eventually returned home but it was a brief stay. After the run in with the train, he was not quite right in the head, so my mother booted him out, which, of course, gave us a one-way ticket back to the 'hood'.

Other events to follow would include my abduction and the subsequent arrest of the kidnapper, when I was taken from a wedding reception, which was somewhat traumatic, as well as being held captive by a group of drunks in a bathroom for twenty-four hours when I was attempting to collect overdue subscription payments from my paper route, and I could go on, but let's try to keep it somewhat pleasant. They had nothing to do with the neighborhood.

At this point you may be asking yourself, why am I reading about this guy's childhood? The answer is that it is my intent to prove to you that, no matter what your upbringing, education, or environment was prior to reading this book, you can overcome adversity and succeed. Dealing with that success is another matter.

If you have had the perfect conditions for success and have the utmost confidence in your abilities, skip ahead to chapter twelve. For all the rest of you, the next eleven chapters tell of the journey from my childhood in Kenosha to my entrepreneurship experiences with seven different business start-ups prior to the drama that occurs with Plan Express and bringing in outside investors that begins in chapter twelve.

I want everyone who reads this book to walk away saying, "If this guy can make it, so can I."

2

Times Were Different Then

I missed most of the third grade after a diagnosis of rheumatic fever. That meant staying home alone, watching the Chicago Cubs on WGN, *Sky King, Car 54,* and other black-and-white TV shows while attempting to study. Upon my return to class, Mrs. Carroll, my teacher, didn't sympathize much, judging by the fact that she grabbed me by the ear and ripped the lobe to the cartilage because I was talking in class. My mother was not very pleased with my teacher's behavior. One day when Mrs. Carroll was having lunch at the restaurant where my mother worked, mom took a bowl of hot soup and dumped it in my teachers lap.. You just didn't mess with my mom.

The rheumatic fever had an impact through much of my life. The weekly blood draws were one thing, but the constant medication and worry of heart problems meant I was not allowed to go to gym class and had to be careful of too much exercise. That ensured I remain a very skinny kid all through school even though many years later with the advent of ultrasound, I learned there was no heart damage.

During my middle school years, I got a job delivering the *Chicago Tribune* and the *Sun Times* every morning before school. That was a decent job for a kid in the summer but pretty tough in the winter. Needing to improvise my clothing to stay warm, I layered socks as mittens and walked around in ski boots borrowed from my uncle. The houses that subscribed to the paper were very far apart and not many people in Wisconsin subscribed to the Chicago papers. My route was from Sixtieth Street to Seventy-Fifth Street and First Avenue to Eighth Avenue. It was quite a hike—by my calculations around thirteen and a half miles.. All that walking ensured that I stayed a skinny 112 pound, five foot, nine inch kid.

My sister and I attended Catholic school all through our grade school years. Back then our first class of the day was the daily Mass service. I enjoyed being an altar boy. I liked wearing the robes and wearing the rope that represented the color of experience and seniority. I remember as a sixth grader being envious of the eighth graders who looked so sophisticated in their gold ropes. I also liked the series of colored metal badges we would receive for being crossing guards. How cool it was when I got the pale blue "captain" badge and could tell the other crossing guards what to do.

Of course there was cub scouts and then boy scouts and all the uniforms, sashes, and badges that went along with that.

One of my most memorable experiences of that time was of the scoutmaster who was going to demonstrate the proper way to cut a log with an ax. We were on one of our overnight trips when, after a lengthy lecture, he proceeded to take a full windup at the log. He was holding it down with his booted foot and he proceeded to swing the ax down onto his big toe, severing half of it. He went into immediate shock as did most of the troop. I stared at the shoe and still have a clear image of it to this day.

I loved the scouts but the combination of the ax incident and some sort of impropriety with him or one of the other leaders broke the pack up. I really don't know the details, but I did hear rumors that are typical of the things you hear more recently having to do with coaches. It was sad to not be able to finish all the electives to achieve Eagle Scout status.

I had a huge secret all the while I was doing "boy" things like scouting and being part of bicycle gang. I also attended ballet school. My mother, was very confident my sister Gena was going to be a famous ballerina, but the instructor said she needed a male dancer to show off her talent. Thus I became a ballet dancer. The classes were at no cost, as the teacher knew our situation and I actually didn't object that strongly, it was fun. What I didn't expect was to see one of the cool girls in my class sitting outside the studio waiting on the next lesson, watching me exit in tights. The shock on her face made me immediately beg her not to tell anyone. She promised she would not. However, the next morning everyone in class was calling me a ballerina. This was worse than being called Alice! I denied it and of course I never went back. In the end, my sister broke her ankle, effectively ending her dancing career as well.

It is hard to comprehend now how long the days must have been then. Up at 4:00 a.m., deliver papers, church at 7:00 a.m., and, of course, we walked to school. Full classes until 3:30 p.m., then detention for almost an hour everyday for talking in class. Attending scout meetings, attending ballet, playing kick the can, doing homework, and building model airplanes, tanks, and cars. Riding bikes, watching *Batman*, enjoying weekends on the farm with the grandparents and Lawrence Welk, and of course, playing priest.

Evil in the Boardroom

The priest thing lasted about a year. I had built a full altar, had sheets for linens, a goblet for a chalice, and Nesbit candies as the communion. Gena was forced to take candy communion nightly and listen to me do the entire Mass. I'm not sure why I was so enthralled, but I had memorized the Mass, including the priest's parts in Latin, and liked to show off my skills, I guess. That all came to an abrupt halt when my uncle Dick heard I was considering the seminary. I truly adored the man and hung on his every word. He let me know in no uncertain terms that his nephew was not going to be a monk walking around wearing a rope. That was that.

Around this time we were at our lowest poverty level. We received food from the county and only shopped at the Goodwill store. Holes in shoes were repaired with cardboard cut to fit, and secondhand clothing seemed new. On one shopping trip to Goodwill for a school coat, my mother purchased a white vinyl number for me that was atrocious, but what choice did I have but to wear it – it was subzero temperatures and it kept me warm. I had just started to participate in sports and had been practicing basketball in the gym. Afterward I went to get my coat out of the locker only to find it wet. I thought it was strange but I had to put it on because it was very cold outside and snowing.

While waiting for my friend Danny to walk home with me, I realized that not only was the coat wet, it smelled, of urine! That was humiliating and pretty uncomfortable. Danny found out who did it and pushed him up against the wall and really tore into him. I never did find out the reason why they had peed on my coat. We hadn't had any altercations or anything. Was it simply because they were from well-to-do families and I was poor. Was that the reason why?

About that same time, my other uncle on my mom's side, Bart, taught me to shoot a bow and to ride a motorcycle and I started to come out of my shell in ways other than just talking during class.

With my two Uncles filling in as father figures, I was very fortunate to have them as my mentors, however, because my uncles were not there on a daily basis, and with my mom working nights we had a lot of time with no supervision. The result of which involved smoking cigarettes, stealing candy, egging cars, vandalizing empty houses, and doing things with young girls that were not condoned

One time when telling my uncle about some of the escapades we'd been involved in he asked if I had ever gotten into a fight. I told him I had been in a few and he asked if I'd won. Back then a fight consisted of punches to the stomach, wrestling and headlocks. I said no, no one really won. When I said that, he told me next time it happened to punch the kid right in the nose.

So about a week went by, and sure enough, a bully named Gary started pushing and teasing me. I immediately slugged him as hard as I could right in the face. He was absolutely shocked. He just looked at me. I walked away, and he never bothered me after that. That new weapon worked very well until the ninth grade and public school.

Going to a public school after eight years of Catholic school was weird, to say the least. The nuns had drilled over and over into our heads about how the public school kids were so much smarter than we were and that we were going to be in big trouble trying to break into the curriculum they had. The nuns were relentless in making us feel inferior.

Evil in the Boardroom

What a shock it was going to my first English class at Lincoln Jr. High. Those kids couldn't read. Science class was the same. How could those fortunate kids with labs and all that equipment and a teacher for every subject be so dumb? The truth in retrospect is that they were not dumb, they just didn't have the quality of education my classmates and I had.

That school year quickly turned very ugly with a good beat down in the parking lot by a school bully that broke my nose and then a gang fight a week later that I did OK in—only to have my nose broken again and straightened by that kid's older brother. It was very segregated back them and this particular time our group of 4 were surrounded by a group of 6 or 8 black kids. We were punched and pushed and I pushed one of the attackers through a glass door. His brother found me that next week. He then semi straightened my nose. The year was filled with riots, rock throwing, gang fights, and threats, following the riots happening in other cities after the Martin Luther King Jr. assassination. That led me to take the rest of the school year off.

There were four or five of us who decided it was safer to skip school and hide out in a friend's garage attic rather than run through the hood to get to school. We started chain smoking, discovered alcohol, and found out that you really can light a fart on fire. Dave, one of our gang, was quite good at that.

We finally got called into the school and were sent to the principal's office to explain our absenteeism. We pointed out that we could not get to school without getting beat up. We had been there just enough to take the important tests, which were extremely easy to pass. They didn't believe our claims of threats and fights and wanted to know who was doing it. We said we didn't know the names, only what they looked like.

Without warning, the principal went on the school loudspeaker and announced to the whole ninth-grade building, "All negro boys are to report to the principal's office now." A line formed outside in the hallway, and we were told to point out the ones who had been threatening us.

You can imagine the looks we got and the anxiety we felt. I decided not to say anything, and so did Dave and Steve. Paul, one of the tougher of my friends, decided to point out some of the offenders. We were told that everything would be taken care of and we were to return to school the next day.

I never went back. About a week later, Paul was beaten up pretty badly. Thank God I only had to go there for one year then it was off to a different high school for tenth grade.

About that time my mother met and married a man named Vic. Vic was an estimator at a plumbing contracting firm, easily the largest shop in town if not the region. Vic was a real businessman in my eyes. He always wore a white shirt and tie, had perfect hair, good looks, and was smart. He even had his own driver. I found out later that was not really a company benefit but a requirement due to some past offenses with driving and drinking. Regardless, that man had a huge impact on my life. My mother and Vic quickly married, and my sister and I moved into a large brick home along with Vic's sons, Jim and Wayne. Yes, it was a bit awkward having Dewayne and Wayne in the same household. Little did I know at the time, Wayne would pretty much be with me for the next thirty-plus years as I would have to deal with his addictions for most of my life as everyone else gave up.

3

Let the Fun Begin

My high school years were a series of adventures that I am not necessarily proud of but never afraid to admit to. I was not a role model by any means. My grades were average at best, except for drafting and shop classes, which were always all As. Trouble seemed to find me, probably because of the friends I chose to pal around with. As an experienced smoker and drinker and not much into sports, after the peeing incident with my coat, I hung out with a tough crowd that wasn't much good at school activities either.

Having been a huge saver since my first job, I would buy only important things. Mother's Day gifts were very important, and I would spend a couple months' savings on a special present. I also saved enough to buy a brand-new motorcycle when I was fourteen. I was able to get a license at fifteen and rode it to school. That was pretty cool as no one else had one.

By sixteen I had an old Nash and my first serious girlfriend, Phyllis. She didn't drink, but I thought it would be cool to take her to the outdoor movie where we could have rum and Coke and hopefully make out. Bad move. She actually passed out in the car. I could not get her to wake up, so I took her to my house.

I went in and told my mom and Vic what had happened, and they helped carry her from the car. My mom called Phyllis's mom and told her that Phyllis had gotten sick from the flu, had a bad vomiting spell, and had fallen asleep. She assured her that everything would be fine and she would get her home in the morning.

Meanwhile, Phyllis did wake up and was vomiting profusely and apparently had other issues due to a time-of-the-month thing. So although my mother covered for us, she was livid. She would help Phyllis for a bit and then come to me where I was cowering in the other room and tear into me like you couldn't believe. You just didn't mess with my mother. As a sixteen-year-old and with my mother now happily married, I no longer got the flyswatter or the belt, but sometimes the verbal tirade was worse. Anyway, it was very sweet of her to tend to Phyllis, and after that incident blew over, they became friends for the next year I was with her.

I held a job at two gas stations and later became an orderly at a nursing home on third shift during the summers. I also bought a '68 Firebird at seventeen. That car brought about a real change in my persona. It was very fast, and I added all the requisite accessories to make it one of the coolest cars in school. I felt better about myself and didn't feel the need to hang around with other people to try to be cool. Even my grades started to get better. I loved driving it, working on it, and taking care of it. It was also how I met my soon-to-be wife.

You need to understand that, at seventeen, I was just shy of six feet tall, weighed 118 pounds, had bad acne, and had long, frizzy, wavy blond hair. I was not very attractive, but I had a really cool car and a newfound feeling of self-worth. This must have been apparent to others because one day as I was attaching my combination lock to my locker, a cute girl with glasses, long hair, a flannel shirt, and tight hip-hugger jeans came up to me and said hi. It was like in a movie when you see the guy look around like she must be talking to someone else.

Yes, I was dating Phyllis and she was attractive, but this girl was different. No one had ever approached me like that before. When I finally figured out she was speaking to me, I somehow managed a "hi" back, at which point she said she really liked my car. Brave me replied "How would you like a ride at lunch?"

Of course she said yes because it was the car she liked, but in time, my personality did win her over. Her name was Sandy, and she ended up moving into our house a year later. Her mother had a serious drinking problem and made her life awful. Sandy became a member of our household and a daughter to my mother. Keep in mind though, that my mother was really conservative and there were separate bedrooms and strict rules.

As I contemplated what to do after high school, I realized that the job of working as an orderly in the nursing home had given me a passion for the medical field. My stepfather and my mom agreed to pay for my books for college if I earned the tuition. I decided that after graduation I would go to the University of Wisconsin/ Parkside and concentrate on science courses to try and become a doctor. My last year of high school was fairly easy, and I had an extra credit and a half, enough to graduate, so I decided to skip Mr. Thomas's architectural drawing class to work more. I was able to work the nursing home job and the gas station job during my senior year and save money for college.

My folks put together a party for my high school graduation, sending out invitations and ordering food and decorations for the celebration. As the day approached, the list of the graduating class was issued. When I went to pick it up and get my cap and gown, I found out that my name was not on the list. Unconcerned, I went to the principal's office to correct the mistake. To my surprise, the principal told me that Mr. Thomas had given me an F, and I was therefore a half credit short from being able to graduate. He suggested that I should enroll in summer school to make it up. I argued that I had been very careful to count my credits and that just could not be right.

"Son," Mr. Fowler said, "you are not on the list of graduates, and you will not be receiving a diploma or attending the commencement ceremony." That was it, case closed.

I was devastated and went home to explain the situation to my mother. She was equally devastated and had to cancel the party. My name was stricken from the list of graduates, and to this day, I must watch for reunions, as my name never makes the list because it is based on the commencement graduates who were there.

A week before summer school was to start, I went to sign up for class. All the records were pulled from my three years of high school to get a definite count of earned credits so I would know what class I needed to sign up for to get the diploma. After sitting with one of the office staff for half an hour, she stood up, grabbed all the paperwork and went into the principal's office. A little while later, the principle came out and conceded that a mistake had been made and that I was actually over by half a credit. He handed over a signed diploma with my name on it, said he was sorry and offered his hand to shake. I ignored it, took the diploma and left.

I missed the first semester of college but signed on for the second, taking classes in biology, anatomy and physiology, math, and chemistry. In between, I applied for and won a job as a lab technician at VR Wesson, making special testing samples for a PhD who was trying to find a better tungsten/carbide mixture for the company. It was a very cool job, although I almost killed myself one night when I blew up a hydrogen/oxygen furnace. I was literally thrown fifty feet and was extremely fortunate to survive. The furnace was destroyed. The lesson here is to pay attention when being taught about mixing and lighting combustible gases. The instructor never told me would could happen if you did it incorrectly.

4

Time to Get Serious

After my near death experience at the lab, I started looking for other work and it was just after classes started that I got a very sought after job on the assembly line at American Motors Corporation. I worked nights at AMC and took classes during the day. It was incredibly exhausting and I had little time to study. I finished the semester with a 3.2 grade point average. It was not good enough to get into a medical school, but I felt that if I could do 3.2 on those tough classes with no studying, I would kick it up a notch and work my way to a higher grade point average the next semester. Being as I was now making a real wage, I wanted to move out of the house. The plan was that Sandy and I would move into a trailer I had my eye on. It was a fourteen-by-seventy-foot, brand-new mobile home with a fireplace. We loved it. When we brought the brochure home to show my mom, she let us know in no uncertain terms that we were not going to shack up together. There was no argument because you just didn't argue with my mother. So it was decided that we would get married. I sold my prized possession, the Pontiac Firebird, and after a very short time, just long enough to pick a dress, set the date, and do the invites, we were married at the nearest church and had our reception at my folks' house. They loaned us five thousand dollars for a down payment on a home, so instead of the trailer, we moved into a house at the end of the block, the day we were married.

So at nineteen years old, I was married, had a mortgage and a full time job and was trying to get straight A's to get into medical school.

Sandy was eighteen and worked too, first at the naval base and then as a teller for the local bank.

I studied during work, between classes, and on weekends and was doing fairly well, except for a bad test in biology. As I left the class that day with the test I had just received a C on, I saw a notice behind a glass display on the hallway wall. "ATTENTION: University of Wisconsin/Madison is now accepting students into the medical program who are of African and/or Hispanic descent with grade point average of at least 2.5." I was crushed. I knew that, as a white American, I had to have 3.8 at a bare minimum to even have a chance at admission, and here I was with a C paper, a wife and a full-time job and I was soon to find out, a baby on the way.

Life didn't seem very fair. I really did not know how I was going to be able to succeed. Should I give up my dreams of becoming a Doctor and just stay in school. What would happen when Sandy couldn't work. How could I make ends meet?

I went back to Vic and asked for advice. I had been helping him do plumbing design work on the side. He would place the fixtures on the drawings, and I would do the drafting to show the piping, venting, and sanitary required for permitting. Vic really liked my work and said I should seek an apprenticeship through the union to become a licensed plumber. That made sense to me, so I went to the union hall, signed up, and took the apprenticeship aptitude test. Based on the test results and my interview, I was number one of sixty-three on the list and I was very excited. This was it, I was on my way.

My very close friend all through school was Hank Garcia. He was dating my sister then, and he had married her recently. He decided to go the same route I had with an apprenticeship. He, too, worked at AMC. Hank was very bright, did well on the test, and ended up sixteenth on the list. A few months later, Hank told me he got the call and was starting at a plumbing company for a five-year apprenticeship. I was dumbfounded, he was #16 on the list and I was #1. How come he had gotten the job and I hadn't? I called the union hall to ask what had happened and found out there were not enough minorities in the union, so until the percentage was brought higher, I would remain at number one. I was really frustrated. Given the current economy and the number of people needed to meet minority standards it was unlikely I would get in the program anytime soon.

With my medical career out of reach and my plumbing career stalled, I decided to take a real estate course and go for a real estate broker's license. That turned out to be quite easy, and at twenty years old, I was working part time evenings and weekends as a broker for a new real estate company in my hometown. I knocked on doors, hosted open houses, and went to seminars.. I was also still working full time for AMC. I ran for union steward for my department and won, becoming the youngest union steward ever at the time.

Evil in the Boardroom

With a little extra money from real estate, we were able to buy baby furniture for our soon-to-be-born son and our first new car, a 1974 Volkswagen Beetle. The price was $3,102. There was a gas crisis in 1974, and we figured that car would help a lot because it had the highest mileage average of any car at the time. Being the smooth negotiator that I was, I offered $2,800 for the car. "I will take this one right here, and pay cash," I told the salesman.

The guy just looked at us and said no. Expecting a counter offer and receiving nothing, I said, "OK, I can go to three thousand dollars, cash." He looked at us and said no. I would bet I was pretty red-faced by then and stupidly said, "Fine, I will pay the $3,100 dollars." He said the price was $3,102.

I jokingly said, "You won't sell this car for a two-dollar discount?" Again he said no. We paid $3,102, plus tax.

I realized that day how important it is to understand the strength or weakness of your position when buying or selling a product of any kind. You look like a fool trying to bargain in a hot market and you can be equally foolish not bargaining when the market isn't as hot.

5

Times Are Changing

The next two years brought us different kinds of changes with the birth of Clint our first son and shortly behind him our second son, Bart. We were the youngest of anyone we knew to have kids and we loved it. However, I was growing tired of my assembly job at AMC but I wasn't making enough money in real estate to do it full time.

I decided to take an aptitude test with the air force and was offered the "Boot Strap" program, which consisted of a full college scholarship with staff sergeant pay while going to school in exchange for an eight-year commitment. The problem was that I really wanted to fly at the time, and they would not guarantee that, so I passed.

AMC, had just announced a thirty-year-and-out pension plan for an early retirement so we decided I should just stick with the company. The kids would be grown while we were still young and with the pension we would go cross-county on a motorcycle, camping out and enjoying life. I took some classes at the community college and applied for a supervisory position at work, as there was no way I could envision being on the assembly line that long. What made things awkward was the fact that I was a union rep trying to get a job on the opposite side. It was customary back then as a union steward to defend a fellow worker in the supervisor's office with dramatic, exaggerated arguments that frequently turned into all-out screaming matches. That proved to your coworkers, who you represented, that you were doing your job, and most of the supervisors went along with the practice.

One day in 1976, things went all wrong. One of those typical meetings didn't seem to be progressing as they normally did. It escalated to involve the chief steward and the general foreman, and finally the superintendent and a union board member joined the fray. This may seem strange but it was customary and a big badge of honor to be fired during these sessions. It was all done with a wink and a nod with everyone understanding it was part of the game and you were never fired in reality. However, on this occasion, it was different. I was fired for insubordination but without the usual wink and nod. As a matter of fact, the general foreman, Harry Rasch, told me in anger that I was nothing and would never be anything. That was his way of ending my dream of a company position. It really hurt my feelings, and I was escorted out of the plant. I did not understand why this turned on me. Perhaps Mr, Rasch had just had a very bad day and took it personal.

The union board member tasked with talking with me said that I would be back on the job in a day or two at the most. I called every day, and the board member told me that the company was fighting hard to keep me fired, but the fact that I had never missed work and was on union duty at the time meant I would prevail.

A week later he didn't sound so optimistic. I panicked. I had two kids in diapers, was living paycheck to paycheck and had almost

21

no savings. I could not get unemployment and didn't know what to do. I called Vic and my mom.

They came over to the house, and we met and went over our options. I decided I wanted to buy a corner grocery store that was for sale or apply for a convenience store franchise. They were supportive and said they would do what they could to help. We had paid back the five thousand dollars we had borrowed previously in half the time, and they knew we had the work ethic to succeed. The next day, however, Vic called me and said he had a friend in the Quad Cities who was running a welding school, and he thought he could get me in. I also received a call that same day from the board member. He said that I could return to my job if I made a personal apology to Harry Rasch. He also said that I would most likely be transferred to another department, thereby losing my union steward position.

That was by far the most critical decision I had ever had to make in my life. The welding school required a minimum of twelve weeks of ten-hour days of training, and it was located a five hour drive away from home. There would be no pay, and we would incur hotel expenses for the entire time with no guarantee of employment at the end of it all. Going back to AMC would secure a pension but would also mean swallowing my pride and basically agreeing that Harry was right and I would never amount to anything. We decided that it was best to not go back to the security of AMC and that a job in the trades would ultimately give us a better life-style and more security in the long run. So off I went to learn how to weld pipe, leaving Sunday nights at midnight and returning at midnight on Fridays. We depleted out savings, sold a car, borrowed some money and went into full cash conservation mode to be able to go on this adventure.

Evil in the Boardroom

Upon graduation from the school, I got a job at the Byron Nuclear Plant near Rockford, Illinois. We sold our house in Kenosha and bought that fourteen-by-seventy-foot trailer with the fireplace and three bedrooms and had it delivered and set up near the job site. I worked in below zero weather, confined spaces, and dangerous positions and loved every minute of it. I was quickly earning much more than the wage I received at AMC and was taking great pride in my welding ability. I was also able to spend a lot of time with the kids, and we enjoyed our new life.

We were there for a little over a year when Vic called to say that a new power plant was going in near our hometown. I called the union hall and was brought in as one of the first workers. We had our trailer moved back to Kenosha and bought a piece of land to build a house on someday. One of the foremen saw some of my welds and asked if I could make a sample to show to our union business agent. I laid down a couple of what we called "coupons," or samples, on six-inch pipe, one 5g (45-degree angle) and one 6g (vertical overhead). They were beautiful.

About a week later, the head business agent came out. He informed me that they had sent my samples to Washington, DC, to the international union, and they had given him the authority to hire me to set up a school similar to the one I had attended in the Quad Cities to teach others how to weld pipe. There was a shortage of qualified welders for all of the power plants under construction. My dream job just got even better. With Fred Eckler, an old hand from the local union, I set up a school in a building on the property and graduated sixty-five welders into the program in over a year and a half. I took the opportunity to bring many of my friends into the school and get them into the trades.

When the needs were satisfied, the school was shut down and I went back to work in the field welding. An opportunity came along where an operating nuclear facility was looking for qualified welders to replace the steam generator nozzles in the containment building at the facility. The job paid foreman scale, would last a minimum of fourteen weeks, and would be thirteen hours per day for seven days per week with time and a half and double time. I took the job and made enough money—over what turned out to be four months—to go forward with building our first home.

After that job was complete, Vic asked me if I wanted to come to work with him. He was going to open his own mechanical construction firm at the age of fifty-nine years. He had gotten bypassed on a promotion at his work and decided to leave and leverage his connections with some money from a partner to start fresh. I started out in the field but quickly came into the office where he taught me how to estimate and bid projects. A year later I was a twenty-seven-year-old vice president and feeling pretty full of myself.

One summer I went back into the field for a two-week shutdown repair we had won.. I was partnered up with my friend Kurt, and our assignment that day was to put up eighty feet of six-inch gas line with hangers over a large furnace. We worked very hard for my stepfather's superintendent, Orville Kelly. I had much to prove. At the end of the day, he looked at our work and yelled at us for not doing more. I was embarrassed and didn't understand, so the next day we decided to show him a thing or two. Our assignment was similar, but we skipped all of our breaks, busted our tails, and put up over one hundred feet. He yelled again.

Evil in the Boardroom

The third day we determined that he couldn't yell at us much more than he had the previous two days, so we pretty much screwed around all day and did sixty feet. Orville looked at the work and yelled again. For the rest of the shutdown we did about sixty feet and got yelled at every day. We'd learned that it did not matter how hard we worked, we'd get yelled at anyway, so why kill ourselves? This was an extremely valuable lesson that I have used as a lesson throughout my life in management. When someone does a good job, tell them so, and when they don't, let them know that too. Clear direction of what is acceptable and what is not is required. I ended up raising my boys with the same principle, and they turned out to be great men.

We went on to build our dream home, put in a pool for the kids, and built a great deck around it. Everything was great for three or four years.

My life was changing and I was being asked to help grow the company by attending association meetings, lodge events, and wining and dining clients and contractors, or I was being wined and dined by various vendors. As a result, I would come home late a couple of times per week. To make up for that, I would try to bring my wife along quite often but while I had been out learning new things and getting exposed to different situations, Sandy had not.

Over the past five years, I had learned a great deal about things Sandy was not familiar with, such as various things to say or not to say in social situations, and I had gotten used to a very different class of people than we were previously accustomed to. Being with these people over the course of the last few years, I was comfortable and Vic had taught me a different lifestyle.

At company functions, I noticed a sense of bitterness from Sandy during conversations, and she overcompensated with criticism and the need to correct me in front of others if I slightly exaggerated a story, which I was known to do from time to time. This does tend to throw off a conversation and can get very uncomfortable. I started to feel that I couldn't be myself at those events so in time, I stopped bringing her along so as to not take me off my game.

That only made things worse at home, and she would use that time to equal up the playing field, and that was the beginning of the eventual end of the marriage. However, for a time, we continued to try and make the marriage work but it was a really rough period of my life.

6

A New Beginning and My First Business

We were beginning construction on our second new home, a real dream house, when a number of events collided. Not only was my marriage crumbling, but Vic pulled into work one day and said he was leaving and moving to Phoenix without my mom. All he said was he couldn't take the badgering anymore, he had found a job there, and that was it. He took off, and I was left to run the business just at a time when all of our industrial accounts stopped outsourcing their construction and maintenance. There was no money in the business and no contracts on the horizon.

We had been looking for jobs through the construction project lead reports and saw that there was a ton of work going on in Phoenix. I also had a cousin who lived there, and her husband was in construction and he said it was sure thing. So my best friend, Randy, who was working for me at the time, and my mom and I decided that we would equally invest in starting a brand-new plumbing company in Phoenix. By mutual agreement, I laid Randy off as we had no work and with our money, he went to Phoenix, with a plan for me to follow as soon as the business could afford me.

I went to the bank and got a business loan for ten thousand dollars. I shut down Vic's business and went to work for a larger mechanical contractor in Chicago while I waited for the Phoenix business to grow. Which it did and very fast. I made five trips there in just over a year, and saw the opportunity for a fresh start and a chance to save the marriage. Sandy and I went down to look for a home in Scottsdale. We found a new home that we wanted and returned to my partner Randy's house, where we were staying. The next morning he asked if we could go to breakfast before we wrote the offer. Over pancakes and bacon, he informed me that he had been the one who had done so much work to get the company to where it was and that he and his wife didn't think it was fair that I just move down to Scottsdale and get the benefit of a salary due to his hard work.

I reminded him that we were equal owners; with my mother, we were, in fact, majority owners. Also, it was my idea, I had helped almost every day, and I would bring in plenty of work to cover my salary. Lastly, it was the deal we made when we started. He said fine, but it wouldn't work and he might even quit. He then told me, "Why don't you just go home, and I will send you a check each year?"

I didn't know what to do so I agreed and we left.

Sandy and I got on the plane dejected, angry, and hurt. That was the final straw on trying to save the marriage. We divorced, sold the house, and went our separate ways. I got the kids every Tuesday and every other weekend and I bought a house two blocks away to be close by. I had hired on with the Chicago Contractor under the pretense that a large chunk of my pay would come in the form of a performance bonus at Christmas. I worked hard and ran quite a few projects, all profitably. The Christmas party was at a posh country club. I was there alone and nervous. The owner came up to me near the end, patted my shoulder saying well done, and handed me a white envelope. I couldn't wait to get to my car to look at the bonus. I opened it up expecting five grand. Ten? No...but three thousand for sure. Wrong again, five hundred bucks. A little note that said what a great year I had and that there was nowhere to go but up from here. I quit on Monday and went to work for an even bigger contractor.

After a time, I was ready to date again and had my eye on my friend Joe's sister, Debbie, who had recently divorced too. To get our first date, I made an appointment at the salon where I knew she was working as a hair stylist, and we hit if off, starting a whirlwind romance. We went on vacations regularly and started to spend a lot of time together. I really enjoyed her family and became a very close friend with her father, Al.

Meanwhile, my mother had started a real estate career in her late forties, as Vic had left her with no money. Not that he took any; they just didn't have much saved. It turned out Vic was a paycheck-to-paycheck kind of guy too. Vic in the meantime, had married a wealthy widow in Phoenix, and I would not see him again for fifteen years. Randy was doing well running our company in Phoenix, but I was having a hard time getting my tax return from him. After a threatening letter from my accountant to Randy, we got the tax return, only to see that there were no profits and he was paying himself $154,000 per year. We had both agreed to work for $40,000 per year. I then commenced a lawsuit, only to find out through discovery that he, in fact, had started a brand-new company and had transferred one million dollars from our company to his new one. It was a long battle but eventually my mom and I got our payout from him.

It was around my first-year anniversary at the larger mechanical contractor, when one of my old acquaintances from Vic's shop called me. He was a small General Contractor or "GC" who was doing about four million dollars in sales. He was thinking about expanding his company into a new construction segment, retail construction and he needed a project manager.

I was rolling along pretty well at the time making $52,000 per year plus a car. I was working as a project manager building numerous high-rises in downtown Chicago. He said he could pay me $40,000 plus a car or $45,000 without a car. It was a huge move backward, but I would be close to home and would not have to commute every day. He also promised me that he would pay a bonus based on profits and that we could put a plan together that everyone would be happy with. I interviewed with the man I would be reporting to and accepted the position.

Everybody thought I was crazy to take a cut in pay. Don Pharr Jr. and his vice president, Gene Sunday, and I began to work together in 1987. The name of the company was State Construction and my new division was going to try building retail stores nationally for the big chains expanding into the regional malls. One of those chains was a retailer called Fashion Bug. Gene had built a Fashion Bug in town and did a nice job on it. The owner then asked if he would build a second store in Madison, over two hours away. Don was reluctant, but Gene wanted to try it.

Evil in the Boardroom

As it turned out, the job in Madison made more money than the local job. Gene had gained a lot of knowledge from the first build and applied it to this job. We worked hard to mechanize the process of building stores farther and farther away and perfected the operations to more and more customers. We started adding up to ten million dollars per year in new sales.

My compensation plan guaranteed that State would make at least $400,000 in profits to offset the payment of my base salary and the overhead and profit associated with it. For every $100,000 in profit above and beyond the $400,000, I would receive an increasing percentage as a bonus starting at 5 percent for the first excess $100,000 and growing to the point of 15 percent for each $100,000 over one million in profit. Because of the profits I was making for the company, I made $90,000 my first year at State and was soon making over $150,000 per year. I never made the company less than one million in profit for the nearly six years I was there.

However, during my last year there, the company did fifty-two million dollars in sales and was going broke.

7

Hard Work and Lots of Ideas

Until that time, I had never had any excess money. As a matter of fact, I always had to juggle to pay bills. Suddenly I was making enough money to pay my bills, buy a new car, and start to build my own home on a lake. I settled the lawsuit with Randy on the courthouse steps, and my mom and I split the proceeds. That was a windfall at the time.

I also invested in my second start-up idea, which I called Expicon, and I hired Debbie to work there. The company was a national permit expediting firm, the first of its kind. I had the idea for it, took it to Don, and asked if he would be interested in doing it together. He had no interest in it.

Once Don Jr. found out that I had started it and was actually doing pretty well with it, he insisted I close it down. I reminded him that I had asked for his permission first and had gotten it and told him that I would not shut it down. He told me to think about it and if I persisted, I would be fired. Gene came to me and asked me to shut it down as well.

I knew it could be a good business and said if they wanted me out of it they should buy it. Don Jr. bought the business to keep me out of it. I took the proceeds and attempted to create a retail chain for start-up number three. The concept was engraved gifts and the chain stores were to be called Inscriptions. Debbie was in charge and we thought things were going good, but we found quickly that the concept would not scale, so I closed it after two years.

I then asked Don Jr. if we could start a national maintenance company. After much discussion I convinced him that I could set it up and run it and not affect the bottom line of my core business. That division did quite well. That four-year period at the tail end of my thirties was the hardest and most stressful work I had done to that point, but I had never enjoyed my job more or had so much fun. The adventures there could warrant a comedy sitcom.

So how could a company grow to be so successful and then go broke? Our division never had a losing quarter. We were always profitable, but one of the consequences of success is what it can do to one's ego. This had happened to me with my first friend and partner Randy, and now it was happening again with my friend Don Jr.

Don would use all of our profits and the anticipated profits to continually upgrade the building, the equipment, and the staff. At one point Don was trying to hire anyone or everyone he competed with. This is a slight exaggeration, but that was his mind-set at the time.

He succeeded in buying out a company in Racine and bringing on the executive staff, including the president. He also tried to hire a former CEO of a Fortune 500 company. Success also increases your bonding capacity and allows you to construct larger projects. That ended up being the undoing of the company. Three large projects were being run by project managers without proper experience. Multimillion-dollar losses were headed our way, and I was sitting on the executive committee and saw the headlights on the train coming to run us over.

Don argued over and over that it would only be a $300,000 to $500,000 loss. He was wrong. In the fall of 1991, my vendors in the retail division were not being paid and no amount of begging could get them paid. Don would take care of his local contractors first, as they were the ones he had to personally deal with. In an effort to help with cash and in an attempt to save the company, which was now faced with over $800,000 in losses on the local work, Gene and I offered, and Don accepted, $500,000 for us to buy Expicon (now called State Permit) and Alert Service, our Maintenance Division. So Gene and I now owned my second start-up and Alert Service was now my start-up number four.

The losses continued to mount, and by Christmas, I spoke to Don Sr., Don's father, and let him know I would be leaving. The retail clients I had garnered, befriended, and serviced over the last few years were giving me ultimatums as the liens from the unpaid subcontractors rolled in. I proactively left to spare the reputation I had earned. I told Don Jr. we would continue to rent office space for the permit business and for Alert, but I had to quit.

He said he understood, and we parted amicably. He still felt he could save the company. He had our cash for the two companies, we were paying him rent, and he no longer had me on the payroll, so he thought he could overcome the losses. I had no doubt that it would fail, as the numbers on the losses on the local jobs were out of control and nothing was being done to stop the bleeding. The truth is Don should have run the jobs himself or asked me to, but he had other personal issues going on at the time and it had big effect on the situation.

My intent at this time was to simply run State Permit and Alert Service and take a well-earned rest.

8

Start-Up Number Five

Two months later Gene called me at home at 8:00 a.m. and asked if he and my former coworker and in-house competitor (from a sales perspective), Kent Moon, could come out to the lake house and talk. I had a feeling I knew what they wanted, and it was quickly confirmed. They were leaving State Construction too, and wanted to know if I would be a one-third owner of a new construction company.

I was a bit reluctant. It was a risk. I was tired, and I still had two companies to run. However, they both agreed that I would be allowed the time to run the others and that it would be a good partnership. I already knew that Gene and I could be good partners and I trusted him implicitly. I was worried about Kent because we were so competitive at State that we rarely talked. He called me "The King" and didn't mean it in a complimentary way.

Our new company was called Lakeview Construction. We each kicked in our cash contribution of $25,000 and got an additional $200,000 from the bank, and we were off. We even rented additional office space from Don Jr. to try to help him, because he still felt he could save State. We did seventeen million dollars in sales our first year and, in addition, endured two customer bankruptcies: one by Zales and one by Merry-go-Round. We still made money. Everything was going as planned. Our second year, 1993, was even better: we did twenty-three million dollars.

9

Start-Up Number Six

In mid-1993, Don laid off one of his last employees, Jim Angelici, who was turning sixty. Jim approached Gene and I and asked if we would invest in a blueprint company that he would run. Jim had previously run our print department at State, among many other duties. We listened to his proposal, and I said I was not interested. We were building a new headquarters for Lakeview, Gene and I owned retail properties in North and South Dakota, plus we had Alert Service and State Permit, and Lakeview itself was growing quickly, but it seemed the economy was being set up for a turndown. As I walked out of the meeting, I said to Jim half seriously that I might be interested if he opened the company in Memphis. He knew why I said that and responded that he would not move to Memphis, so the conversation was over.

The significance of Memphis came to light a couple of weeks earlier at about four in the afternoon. I could hear phones ringing unanswered all over the place. I got up and went to our print room to see most of our staff stuffing FedEx tubes, printing labels, printing transmittals, and printing plans. I was outraged. There were over twenty superintendents in the field and dozens of customers and hundreds of sub-contractors (or subs) out there not being taken care of. I asked why everyone was back there. It was explained to me that the FedEx pickup was at 5:00 p.m. and we had nearly one hundred packages going out to subs for bids.

I looked at the labels and noticed most of the packages were going to Chicago, sixty miles away. I knew the need to get the plans to the subs the next day. They didn't have much time to begin with to get us a good bid, but why so early for so near? Here was the problem: The plans would fly from Milwaukee to Memphis and then be reloaded on a plane at midnight and flown to Chicago. So the big revelation was that if we could print in Memphis, we could do the work after hours and be much more productive during the day. Our pickup time might be as late as 11:00 p.m. Add to that the fact that now the flight was a one-way instead of a round trip, and we could presumably save a bunch on shipping costs.

About a week after Jim's initial proposal, he returned to the office with a new proposition that, if Gene and I would invest with him, he would move to Memphis and do all of our printing and shipping from there. The company, which we temporarily called Planex, would also solicit other contractors to do the same service for them. It was a good idea and Gene and I signed on. We drew up the agreement on the back of a letter-size envelope, using Gene's trademark green felt tip pen.

We opened in December 1993 and named the company Plan Express. Jim moved there, and I wrote up a marketing letter to my retail clients explaining the benefit to them and their contractors. We picked up five or six retailers immediately and were off to a great start.

A few weeks later, I was shocked and annoyed at my own igno-rance. The retailers were faxing us letters from their contractors saying there was no way they were going to use a service that required them to share their subcontractor information with a competitor. It was common knowledge that Gene and I owned Lakeview Construction. This was not going to work. The only good thing was that Lakeview was growing so fast that our com-pany could probably carry Plan Express alone. We really had no other choice, and Jim needed the work. Of course the other option was for Gene and me to bow out of the company to avoid the conflict of interest.

With all that I had previously mentioned as a reason to not invest in Plan Express, I was now in even deeper. Doing very well, but facing forty and feeling as if I really had done all I wanted to do, I now looked to get that rest I almost earned two years prior. I approached Gene and asked if he would have any interest in buy-ing me out. He was surprised, but I think he knew it was coming. The surprising part for me was how fast he put together a buyout that was reasonable and fair, but that is how Gene Sunday is. He bought Lakeview Construction, Alert Service, State Permit, the properties in the Dakotas, and my portion of the new headquar-ters. It was all fair.

When I looked at the list of assets, I saw that he had not addressed Plan Express. I asked him what he would pay for it, and he said he didn't want it. I said, "Just give me anything and you can have it."

His retort was, "I tell you what, I will gift you my shares in Plan Express to sweeten the deal."

Evil in the Boardroom

I realized that, as a "former" owner of Lakeview, I might be able to market Plan Express once I created a little time and distance. So we did the deal, and I retired. Over a million in the bank, house almost paid off, car and motorcycle paid for, and full pay for two more years. Life was good. Both of my sons were in college and had moved in with me. My girlfriend, Debbie, was promoted at her job and made good pay and traveled the world. It was time to rest, catch up on all my favorite authors, and enjoy the fruits of my efforts.

10

Start-Up Number Seven: Call of the Wild, Are You Kidding Me?

One full month of reading, riding motorcycles, and drinking in the afternoon convinced me that my new plan was not going to work. I was bored silly.

I came up with the idea of a high-end motorcycle boutique to take the Harley comeback phase to the next level. It was June 1994, and the Harley fad was in full swing. There were waiting lists for bikes, and people were paying thousands over list price to get one. I had considered a bike shop right out of high school in partnership with my Uncle Bart. We almost did it, but my uncle Bart wasn't happy with me when I showed him a partnership agreement. He said we didn't need paperwork. Even back then I knew I shouldn't proceed without a signed partnership agreement, so it was off to college instead pursuing that medical degree. The idea now was to build a very cool design, using a retail architect and incorporating some wild ideas I had, such as the world's largest Harley dashboard hanging from the ceiling, a buffed leather look to the floors, and tons of other things that were not yet being done.

Evil in the Boardroom

I did a complete business plan, got a bank loan, found the real estate, designed and built the store, bought the Point of sale and Inventory management software, set up all the vendors and merchandise, and opened by Thanksgiving. My son Bart asked if he could take a year off from college to help me, and I agreed as long as it was just one year. We opened the store, Call of the Wild, obtained an Illinois motorcycle manufacturer's license (never done before at that level), and started building custom motorcycles under the Ellis Motorcycle brand. We bought out a competitor in town who had a machine shop, had a race team, and built the motors.

Within six months of opening, we were breaking even. We were having fun. My first chopper won best of show at the Sturgis Bike Show, and we invented the world's first digital mirror with all the components for speed, turn signals, idiot lights, and odometer behind the mirror. Everything was going according to plan. The problem was it was so great that everybody else wanted to do it too. In less than a year, two shops of similar style opened in a five-mile radius of our store. When we were just moving into profitability, we quickly saw our revenue cut in half. Having more stores did not produce more customers, it only cut into the market I had. For the next year and a half, I lost about $20,000 a month. We outlasted the Easyrider franchise store, and the losses were reduced. With the increased revenue from its closure and also by changing our model to more service- oriented business and parts, we were surviving but relying heavily on my checkbook.

I was no longer having the fun we had in the beginning. My son and I were working all the store hours and dealing with a few employees who were frustrating, to say the least. Our customer base ranged from bikers with no money to doctors and lawyers who put on leather coats and turned into jerks. These were not the majority, but enough of a percentage to ruin my lifelong hobby as a motorcycle enthusiast.

I had found out that the remaining competition was owned by a wealthy, well-known businessman who didn't need the money and had no intention of closing. I decided to approach his business managers to see if they would be interested in buying me out. After a six-month negotiation and courtship, I sold the business and agreed to stay on for one year. I agreed to take the bulk of the payments over time because the company buying me was owned by this fairly famous rich businessman. The actual payout agreement turned out to be a mistake. The new buyer later stiffed me on the final payment which was in excess of $20,000.

Relieved that the deal was complete, I worked very hard over the next several months to ensure the transition was successful. Even though Bart had come a long way in two years, the Business Managers put in their own management team, but Bart would stay on to ensure everything continued as planned. Bart had wanted to go back to college as originally planned, but that was just when everything started to go badly and it was my turn to ask for a favor. He agreed to stay on for another year.

With the transition finally winding down, I had some newfound freedom that coincided with Debbie's employer going bankrupt. It was the opportune time to settle down and marry. We thought maybe we would open a dive shop in the islands or buy a catamaran and do day trips.

Evil in the Boardroom

On May 17, 1997, with Debbie's dad, Al, as my best man and her sister Karen as her bridesmaid, we were married. We left the next morning for a two-week honeymoon to Kauai. Two close friends joined us the first week on the dry side and another couple joined us on the rainy side for the second week. We all had a very nice time.

During the last couple of days of the honeymoon, I found myself in moderate pain from cramps similar to a colitis type of problem I had had since I was fifteen years old.

We returned home to pick up our new puppy, Cody, a golden retriever, and I was going back to the Call of the Wild bike shop for my last few months. On my first day back at work, I noticed a sharp pain in my abdomen as I approached the shop. Throughout the day the pain got worse, but I was accustomed to it from previous bouts over the years. This time was different, though, because when I went to drive home I could not use my right foot for the brake. I couldn't lift it off the gas pedal without extreme pain. By the time I got home, I just wanted to lie down. I could do nothing but kept hoping it would get better. It didn't. At dawn, I asked Debbie to take me to the emergency room. After a quick diagnosis, it was determined that my appendix had ruptured and I had peritonitis.

Surgery was performed, and I was told I would be hospitalized for a week to ten days to kill the bacteria with high doses of antibiotics. It was later the next day when my doctor and the surgeon came in the room to let me know there was nothing wrong with my appendix. I was highly toxic, but not from a ruptured appendix. More tests would be done after the infection was brought under control to determine what was wrong.

45

After twelve days in the hospital, I was sent home and told to schedule a colonoscopy, which I did for later in the week. I was doing the prep of drinking a gallon of Golitely liquid. This was not a pleasant experience, as you must evacuate completely within a 4 to 5 hour timeframe. After the last round, the severe pain I had felt a couple of weeks before returned. Again, back to the emergency room, admitted for another ten days of antibiotics to kill another infection. I was sent home with some oral meds to prep for a CAT scan instead the next week.

I started to feel really lousy but went for the test. I was getting dressed to leave after the procedure when the technician told me to go and pick up the phone. It was my doctor. They were admitting me back in the hospital for the third time for emergency surgery in the morning. He explained that I had three large cysts that must have formed from a leaky colon and all the antibiotics I had received over the last four weeks. I was whisked to a room and given a regimen of enemas and more antibiotics. My intestines were severely swollen and it was extremely painful.

Later that afternoon, the surgeon came into the room to explain the situation. He told me they would be removing at least twelve to fifteen inches of my colon and removing all surrounding organs, including my intestines, to peel away the cysts and adhesions. They would then put it all back together inside me, connect a colostomy bag, which could be permanent but usually was used only for six months, and then reconnect the intestines with another surgery.

I told him I did not want the bag, but he said there was no choice. Debbie was there asking questions as well, but the doctor ignored her at first. When she persisted, he finally told her he would only answer my questions. He was very direct and very unfriendly. I emphasized that I did not want a bag. He went on to say that, if during surgery one of the cysts ruptured, there were not enough antibiotics on the planet to save me. I would die on the table. I asked him what were the chances of that happening, and he said I was lucky to have him because he was the best but there was no guarantees. I again asked if there was anything he could do to hook me back up without the colostomy, and he said I could try doing enemas with large bags of benadine and massive oral antibiotics, and if I was perfectly clean he might attempt it.

We called the pastor who had married us just two months before. He came over and prayed for me through the bathroom door while I was tortured being unable to evacuate during the cleansing process. I became very sick and feverish and could not empty the enemas because of the swelling. I was in tremendous pain. I made peace with God and was prepared to die; I just wished that it didn't have to be so painful. The years of stress and probably bad genetics had destroyed my colon.

I went into surgery for an eight- to nine-hour procedure and awoke in the recovering room to see Dr. Pacanowski sitting at the table writing notes. I asked, "Do I have a bag?" and he replied no. The next time I awoke, I was in a room with Al on my left and Debbie on my right.

Opening my eyes to see them smiling at me, I instantly felt as if I had been run through with a sword and disemboweled and I let out a scream the likes of which I had never uttered before. The nurses rushed in and injected more Demerol, which knocked me out, but then I awoke a few minutes later with the same agony.

That went on three or four times until the anesthesiologist came to the room and added Turgitol to the mix. It was instant relief. Now I just felt as if I had been run over by a truck. I was quite a sight to see, with tubes coming out of six places on my body. My stay there was nearly two weeks. It would take me a month to be able to go out and about and a year before I could say I was anywhere near normal.

11

A New Adventure

After recouping at home and starting to enjoy my puppy, who was now seemingly a teenager, I contemplated what to do next. I was certainly handicapped for the time being, as the healing process would take at least ten weeks and my body would have to adjust to the lack of a colon. I had become friends with a customer from Call of the Wild named Scott. He was a great guy with a wonderful sense of humor, very successful, and a recovering addict. I thoroughly enjoyed his companionship and his funny stories. Scott called me on a Sunday morning and asked if he and his wife could swing be the house to visit.

They arrived, and we sat on the back porch, drank coffee, and had breakfast on a beautiful September morning, overlooking the lake and the change of colors in the surrounding trees. He asked me what I was going to do next, and I said I really didn't know. Scott said he was very impressed at how fast and how well I had put together Call of the Wild, and he knew about some of my previous start-ups, so he had an idea that could help the two of us. He explained that he had acquired five small companies that had starting buying raw materials for their product from his competition. He bought the companies just to keep them from using the competitor's product, but they were not making money. One in particular was giving him heartburn. The operation in Dallas was one he had no control over, and the management in place was running it as their personal piggy bank. Scott said he would give the business to me and I could pay for the equipment over time as long as I continued to buy his raw material. That sounded really good other than the fact of having to move to Dallas, but overlooking that fact, I was certainly up to looking at it more.

He said, "Great, let's go tomorrow."

I said, "OK, how are we going to do that?"

He called his travel person and said, "I need two first-class tickets to Dallas in the morning."

Done.

I went to Dallas the next day, toured the facility, and met the management. Scott had brought all the financials on the plane, which I studied on both segments of the trip. By the time we landed back in Chicago, I knew that it could not work. The sales volumes were good, but there was little chance of a price increase, because the end price was fixed by the retailers. The raw material cost was Scott's price to the division and could not be any cheaper. The rent was reasonable. The only place to change the margin was in the labor cost. The company was not overstaffed other than slightly at the highest levels but not enough to make it profitable by substitution.

My only chance to make money with this gift would be to earn the salary that the current manager received. Of course, I could have relocated the company offshore as I suggested Scott should do, but I was not up to the task. I politely declined the opportunity and thanked him for thinking of me.

Scott called me a few days later and asked if I would be willing to act as a consultant and put together a recommendation for the board. He wanted me to observe all of his small operations and make some recommendations on what they should do. He agreed to pay me a very nice sum for the two weeks I told him it would take. I studied the individual financials of the five locations and interviewed many of the managers as well as some of Scott's other senior management team. I put together a presentation to show that by combining all of the manufacturing into a single facility the companies could breakeven. I also showed an alternative plan where profits could be made under the assumption that the work could be done cheaper in Mexico.

After the presentation, Scott asked if I could put together a business plan for the relocation to Mexico and said he would pay me at the same rate for the new plan if I could provide a comprehensive plan with full budgets within sixty days. I agreed to do the job, although the thought of moving jobs to Mexico was not something I was fond of. I expressed that to Scott, but he let me know that the investment to consolidate in the United States was not worth doing and jobs would all be lost anyway. Moving to Mexico would at least save the managers.

I visited six cities in Mexico to interview numerous contract labor providers, vendors, and developers and put together the plan that I presented to the board just shy of the sixty days. The move would cost nearly one million dollars but would return the investment within one year after completion of the moves.

The board, which included his CFO, looked everything over and asked me if I would be interested in running the project. I said I probably would.

Scott said great but that I had to do it with $600,000. I said I would not be interested in doing that because it was not possible. He asked if I would do it with an $800,000 budget, and I said no again and that I was confident in my numbers. I admitted there might be some room, as I had been conservative in some of my projections. I was given the go ahead to run the project with a one-million-dollar budget and a one-year timeline. I would also get a bonus if I came in under budget. The pay was very good, and the bonus for being under budget and getting it done on time was 50 percent on top of the salary. I was very excited to take on the project but also very nervous. It was a bit beyond my scope.

That was at the beginning of 1998, and my son Clint had graduated from college and moved out. He was the first person in my entire direct family tree to graduate from college. Bart was terminated by the new manager at Call of the Wild, which was a dumb move by them but would work to both of our advantages later. It was also the time when Vic showed back up with a phone call after a fifteen-year absence to ask if he could court my mom again now that his rich wife had just died. That threw my mom into a tailspin that would forever change her. She absolutely panicked when I told her Vic wanted to see her. She cried and pleaded with me to help her avoid him. I told Vic it just wasn't going to work, she would not see him, and he should forget about her. My mother had worked very hard the last fifteen years and had done very well. She did not need anything emotionally or financially from Vic.

Evil in the Boardroom

You could say I was a bit shocked when I returned from a trip to Mexico just a few weeks later to find them holding hands in my living room, but it's even harder to explain my utter bewilderment when they were married two months after that and announced they were going to move to Florida. I knew something was wrong, but I wasn't sure what it was. I called her employer, whom I knew and her close friend, to ask what they thought. I found out that she had double booked some appointments, missed some meetings, and forgotten some birthdays. That was a major red flag for me. My mother was always very organized and sharp. She was only sixty-one years old, so I attributed it to stress and hoped that retiring and relaxing in Florida would make everything normal.

I was commuting to Mexico during the negotiations with the labor provider I had selected. While going over the building design with the developer, Scott asked if I would consider relocating, as the cost of commuting was becoming a bit too much. I had always wanted to eventually move to Arizona and this seemed like the right opportunity to finally get out of the cold. I was forty-four years old, freshly married, and had no ties other than my sons. We decided to move to Scottsdale, and I would drive to work in Nogales, Senora, early on Monday and return on Friday for the balance of the project. I sold the lake house and Debbie and Cody and I moved into our new home in November 1998. It was a great house in a fantastic neighborhood.

Building a 123,000-square-foot building and relocating over two hundred machines along with the hiring and training of two hundred plus employees was quite a chore. I completed the project in just over ten months, and the total cost was just over $700,000. I had been able to work many amenities into the construction

53

budget and the rent on the building. We had a state-of-the-art water purification system, a beautiful cafeteria, twin waterfalls at the entrance, and numerous other upgrades that made for a world-class production facility. When Scott toured the project at the grand opening party, he was ecstatic. I received my full bonus, and he asked me to stay for at least another six months to train the plant manager and to fine-tune production.

I was conflicted at the time. Jim was again asking for my help with Plan Express, but I was in love with the Mexican work force and the community, and I liked the job. However, it was also the height of the dot.com era, and I felt I might be missing an opportunity elsewhere. I told Scott I would stay for another month or two to get the new manager trained but that I really wanted to run my own company again. He understood but really wanted me to stay on. We looked at a few other companies that we could possibly own together but never found anything that would work.

One thing about working in Mexico is the importance of understanding the people and their values, along with their ethics and customs. The culture in Mexico is very different from America and must be understood in order to succeed there. An example is that it is customary to shake hands with every man and kiss every girl's cheek when greeting them. It would be a problem if I were to enter the production area and not do that to everyone in the vicinity.

My HR director showed up in my office one morning with five women. They wanted to file a grievance because I had not kissed them earlier. I had gone to their department and was interrupted by a page, so I went to my office for the phone call and didn't come back out. The dispute was quickly put to rest with a kiss to the cheek and an "I'm sorry" to the five.

Another unique quirk was that if I were to ask a male employee why he wasn't making quota or why his quality was bad, he would not be there the next day because he would have quit. But if I asked him if everything was OK at home, and if he replied yes, why do you ask? I could then say, I noticed your work was not as good as before, so I thought there might be a problem at home. That was acceptable and was one of many things that had to be understood in order to work successfully with the Mexican staff. They are very proud people.

There are good books on the subject that go into the psychology of the Mexican people and why they are so different from any country on earth. I thrived there, and the day I left for the final time was one of the toughest days of my life. I was thrown a party and felt love from a group of people that cannot be explained. I cried the entire four-hour drive home.

12

Plan Express – The Good

It was now August 1999, and I was calling on customers for Plan Express and fascinated by what was going on with the Internet and the companies being created around it. I often wonder what would have happened if I had not taken the job in Mexico. Would I have been one year ahead with my new quest to make Plan Express an Internet company and therefore participated in the bubble? Would it have made a difference in the eventual outcome?

I started soliciting the services of Plan Express full time. The company consisted of Jim, me, and four other employees. We were doing around $400,000 in sales, with the majority of the sales coming from one customer, my old company, Lakeview Construction. It had been five years since I had sold it, and my first calls were to the companies that had initially objected to the concept. When they asked me how they could be secure knowing that their info would not be shared with my old company, the answer was simple. One, I would derive no benefit in sharing a contact, and two, I would be out of business.

I was fortunate enough to double sales in a few months and was trying to figure out how a company that took orders via fax, then printed construction drawings on paper, and then mailed them out via FedEx could be an Internet play. It wasn't as if we had content that could be placed online and ordered; it was each individual customer's content. And even if it were done online, the files were huge at one megabyte each, while a set of drawings could easily be one hundred megabytes. Internet speeds were 56k for most users, and AT&T was charging $1,000 per month at the time for a T1 line. That didn't really didn't matter, because even if the contractors had a T1, it was dedicated to voice traffic, and their subcontractors surely would not have the bandwidth.

Also during the late fall of 1999, another former customer of Call of the Wild whom I had befriended moved to Scottsdale. He was doing a start-up and had asked me to invest in it. The concept was that he would take a car shopper's information and interest in an automobile from an Internet inquiry and send the info to a salesperson for instant callback via an early RIM (Blackberry) device. I really didn't have the motivation to invest in it., I knew that I was going to have to infuse some cash into Plan Express as soon as I could figure out what to do. I shared my idea with him and he suggested I secure venture capital. He knew of a good attorney that would assist me with introductions and advise me with securing the venture capital funding.

I reached out to his contact, Robert Kant of Greenberg/Traurig. Calling and introducing myself, I let him know I might be interested in seeking funding for my company to become an Internet player. He asked if I had a business plan yet, and I said it was still conceptual but that I would send him a rough draft when it was completed. He said he looked forward to seeing it.

I gave Jim, my partner, a call and told him we needed to raise at least one million dollars and turn Plan Express Incorporated (PEI) into an Internet company. He was furious. We had both just started taking a nice wage from the company due to the increased sales from my recent efforts, and it was his opinion that I should keep selling and we could make a lot of money with the company. I shared my thinking that if we didn't do my idea, someone else would, and it could render our company irrelevant. We were now 50-50 partners because I had given him stock when I decided on doing the Mexico project in exchange for him pretty much going it alone during that time. We were at an impasse.

Another huge decision had to be made. The Internet was on fire, my friend from Scottsdale with the RIM device idea had just received two term sheets (Venture Capital interest to invest) in one week for a twenty-five million dollar valuation on a company that didn't even exist, and I couldn't get Jim to agree to raise money by bringing in venture capital. At one point he did say we could do it ourselves, but I knew that would be impossible, as it was going to require quite a bit of money. I called him one last time to try to convince him to get on board, and he said no way, at which point I asked him to buy me out. I was also considering going into residential construction in Scottsdale and would pursue that.

He liked that idea and asked how much it would take to buy my half of the business. I told him that he should pay $500,000 for it based on my salary of $100,000 times five years that he wouldn't have me to pay, so it could go toward the purchase. He thought my price was ridiculous and should be more like $100,000 cash. I remained firm in my asking price, and he just said no.

Evil in the Boardroom

When I pressed him on it he said if I really thought the company was worth that much I should buy him out for that much. I asked why he would think that the company was worth $500,000 if I was buying him out but not worth $500,000 if he was buying my stake. He had no answer for that. I then asked if he would buy me out for $400,000, and he again said no.

I was really on the fence at that point because the housing market was booming and there was a shortage of good builders. I hadn't fully figured out what I would do with PEI, and I was not a whiz when it came to technology. Our conversations were becoming contentious and it was increasingly difficult to talk with him about anything. He was hypercritical of me in every aspect of my interactions with the company. In the heat of another argument over a newsletter, I told him I would pay him $400,000 to sell his half. He said fine, but he didn't really believe me. I assured him I meant it and would have the agreement drawn up by our corporate attorney. I hung up the phone wondering what I had just done. I knew now that I had to get to work on transforming PEI. I needed to raise the money to pay for the implementation of whatever the process would become—once I figured out what that transformation would be.

Writing up the contract for the buyout took a great deal of work on my part. I wanted a loan for half of the amount and it took some effort to secure that. Once presented with the actual contract for the buyout, Jim decided he needed more. I was not happy about that at all and almost walked away, but by then I was formulating the process for the move to the Internet. I was deep into the business plan, and it was starting to look good. Jim wanted the whole $500,000. I felt forced to give it to him. I knew he would not buy me out and I was motivated more than ever and I needed Jim to get out of the way. I agreed to pay him the extra $100,000 in the form of weekly payments for the next two years. We scheduled the close for my birthday in mid-March 2000, and the dot-com companies were at their peak.

I sent my first draft of the plan to Bob Kant. He called me the very next day and asked if I would be interested in coming to a dinner with some of his contacts. This was to be followed by a Phoenix Suns game in the corporate suite and then talking a little bit about the company and my plans for it. Of course I said yes, and the next Tuesday night I was sitting at a table for an early dinner with Bob and at least ten other gentlemen. Bob welcomed everyone and asked each person to introduce himself and share with everyone what he did.

I was ill prepared, so I decided to just explain the core concept of the business: late night ordering and shipping from the Memphis hub and that I was working on bringing it to the Internet via an online plan room. There were a number of other entrepreneurs there as well as bankers, venture capitalists, and consultants. I was excited but felt a bit out of my league. I had never been involved in that type of financing structure before. We caravanned to the arena and enjoyed the game from the suite along with more food and drink.

Not much happened until one of the guys from dinner asked me if we could talk for a minute. He said his name was Dean Woodman (now of GoPro fame) and that he wanted to hear a little bit more about the company. I told him what I could and that I was in the midst of writing the plan but was not sure what to do with it once it was done. He said he would be willing to help me finalize it and make some introductions in the San Francisco area where he had a lot of contacts. I asked him if there was a fee for doing something like that, and he explained that the fee was typically 8 percent of the raise in the form of options plus expenses and probably a board seat with an accompanying stock grant. I said that sounded great even though I had no idea what it meant. I found out later that a raise is the amount of funding you're requesting and options are the right to convert them to stock in the company at a pre-determined price. I returned home jubilant and stayed up all night working on the plan.

I was also working with the bank on a $200,000 loan to buy Jim out and felt that I really needed to get that done. The bank had committed to the loan, but one week before the loan close, they told me I had to put an additional $100,000 into the business and give them a second mortgage on my home. That was not what I had planned for and would require me to come up with $300,000 in cash and still carry Jim's wage and the bank debt. I was moving forward, but with some trepidation. I thought it was very unprofessional for the bank to change the deal like that, but I would find out later how much worse they could actually be.

The NASDAQ had fallen 10 percent in one day, but the Internet was still hot. I closed on the bank loan and then signed the contracts for Jim, cut the check for $400,000, and scheduled the close to take place at my attorney's office in Kenosha. I was in California for my birthday and used my friend's office for the conference call, which was a mere formality. As my attorney passed the check to Jim, Jim slid it back across the table and said it was not enough. He wanted another $100,000 and would take it as a wage, for a total of $600,000.

I was floored. I could not even speak. After a few moments of getting my blood pressure under control, I told Jim to take the check and rip it up so I could hear it and that the deal was off. I said I had no interest in buying the company and that Gene B, the attorney, should take back the contract. After some silence Gene informed me that Jim had signed the contract. I was happy but also sad that he had done that to me. He would later go on to convince Lakeview to buy a print machine from a company he went to work for so they would not have to use PEI for all their work. Here was a lesson to include a non-compete next time. I was able to convince them to stay with us even if it meant me buying the machine from them.

I returned home, made sales calls with renewed vigor, and finished the plan, which was forwarded to Dean in San Francisco. He returned it with some modifications and a contract for the deal between him and me, and said he would get to work setting up meetings.

Once I was fully in control of the business, I needed someone to run the day-to-day operation and take over for Jim. That would be an additional expense, but it gave me the chance to reengage my son Bart who had helped me at Call of the Wild.

Bart had eventually been terminated from Call of the Wild and for the last year and a half, he'd been working at Radio Shack as a store manager. Excelling at the job, he was not only the youngest and best in the district but also high up in the regional stats. He had undergone management training, and I could see a huge difference in his overall skills. He was extremely timid at Call of the Wild except when arguing with me. We nearly came to blows a couple of times, but the reasons for all the arguments were for things he now understood. Jim had not given the key personnel any vacations for the last three years. If any one of those employees were to quit, it would have resulted in a major problem.

I asked Bart if he would come back to work for me. I let him know that he would be my number one go-to guy and that I would give him stock options in the company. I promised to also pay him well and give him raises as the company grew. I shared the vision of the Internet play and the potential for a huge payoff. If it wasn't for the fact that he was tired of the weekends and long hours required in retail, he may not have gone for it. Little did he know how hard he was about to work. The first task was to learn each person's job and then get them caught up on vacations. Knowing I had someone I could trust down in Memphis allowed me to solely focus on sales and getting the company funded.

I started going to San Francisco in May or June of 2000 almost once a week. The appointments at the VC's offices rarely happened on the same day. Dean and I presented to at least twelve different companies and had not received a term sheet.

He suggested that, based on the feedback, a gray hair was needed, meaning that the investors wanted to see someone older and more experienced. We found such a person in John, a friend of Bob Kant's. He agreed to present himself as the company COO and would do so for a wage and 4 percent to 7 percent of the company in the form of options. I said I would go for no more than 5 percent, and he said not to worry, we could make that work. I agreed, and he said we would sign a contract once we received the funding. Now there were three of us on the road doing our presentations to another dozen investors with still no luck.

Looking back, I don't believe anyone was getting funding from any firm at the time. The stock market tech stocks were in free fall. In September Dean let me know that he didn't think we could get the deal done. We were looking for five million dollars at a thirty-million-dollar pre money valuation. Pre money means the value of the company before the investor adds his investment. Under this scenario the company would have a 35 million dollar post money valuation. It wasn't his fault we couldn't get it done, and I know he believed in the business.

At that point he asked if I could make a go of it with one million dollars. Dean was confident he could get some wealthy friends to pass the hat and come up with the money. I said I could do it, and he put the "A" round together very quickly. There was some due diligence required, which took a few months, and the conditions were two board seats for the group, plus John coming on as COO for a third seat. The valuation was proportional to before, just for less. It worked out to one million dollars with a pre money valuation of seven, giving the company a total value of eight million dollars. I was only giving up approximately 15 percent of my ownership.

While that was coming together, I had hired a firm to write the software for our conversion to an Internet-based company. We had a website at the time, but my plan for the back end was laid out for the developers. The specs were for a new, slick front end with a log-in that would take the user to his own private plan room where the drawings would be stored and made viewable and available to order.

The order placed by the general contractor would create an automatic job ticket for the large-format plans to be sent to the digital printers as well as create a shipping label and a transmittal for the recipient. Nothing like that existed at the time, and the company hired said they could do it and have it ready for a huge trade show I had signed up to debut at.

When the deadline came, they delivered only a front-end five-page website. I asked where the log-in was and the plan room, and they said their quote did not include the back end even though it was clearly spelled out. That was a tense time for all, the software company was going bankrupt. I was able to convince the owner to at least give me a DVD of screen shots I could use for the show. It is kind of funny in hindsight, but at the time I was in my booth at the largest convention to ever hit the construction industry, the AEC show, and I was performing demos and clicking on the screen as if we were connected to the Internet. A few people asked what the whirling noise was when I clicked, and I said it was just the computer working hard. Oh my.

We closed on the series "A" round in December 2000. Sales were going to surpass one million dollars, and I had just hired my own team to write the software internally. While at the attorney's office for the close of the funding, I once again had a bit of a double cross thrown at me. One of the documents to be signed was for John's options, as it was a requirement that he be on board for the check to be turned over. As I looked at the stock option grant for John, I saw that it was for a full 7 percent ownership of the company instead of the 5 percent we had agreed on. That was over $200,000 more shares of stock than had been agreed to.

I pointed it out to my attorney, and he said that was what John wanted and that the deal was contingent on me signing off on it. I told John right there at the table that it was not our deal and very unfair. He told me to take it or leave it. I took it because I had to, but it changed the respect I had for him from that point forward. Another lesson learned the hard way. A real pattern was developing here.

I brought on my first salesperson Michelle and a key manager Woodie just before the funding and hired two more salespeople and my controller Amy just after funding. By September 2001, we had grown the company sales by another million dollars without the website being up yet.

September 11th is Bart's birthday. We had a home we bought together in Memphis. I was commuting every other week to Memphis and went in to work early, and he worked late. That morning my salesgirl Michelle called me and told me to quickly turn on the TV. I saw the first tower of the World Trade Center burning and ran to Bart's room, pounding on the door and telling him to get up. He thought I was just trying to say happy birthday at first, and we then watched the rest of the tragedy together.

Our business was instantly closed down. No flights meant no shipments. During the next week, contractors used other local methods, and many projects were put on hold. We were dead in the water. Once things started to settle, we had to resell some of our customers again. By early 2002, we were running short of cash. We had spent a large portion on salaries for the programmers who, by that time, numbered four. We had four salespeople, an accounting department, and a server room with never enough equipment in it. The five-month dry spell really took a toll.

I had kept John away as much as possible to not only avoid paying him, but also because I had to spend a great deal of time getting everyone calmed down after he came to the office and disrupted the staff. With circumstances being what they were, I needed him to conduct a board meeting to figure out how to cover the shortfall in cash. I did not want to lay off any people, because I knew it was a temporary situation. On the conference call with the investors, we explained the situation and said that we needed around $100,000 to get through the cash crunch.

The board member representing one of the investors was a guy from Colorado named John G. He was not an investor but was married to one of the investor's sisters. He worked for a large contractor and was the investor's industry expert. When his brother-in-law asked John G what he thought, he went on to give a big speech about the state of the market and about how PEI had yet to prove the business model would succeed. I immediately asked him why he would say such a thing when we had doubled sales in spite of such an unforeseeable event. The investor whose name was Tim decided to dress me down, as they say. How dare I challenge a statement made by their expert? I then let them know that he was obviously not much of an expert at anything because he couldn't even back up his statement with any facts. I left the room at Dean's request as it was not going well at all, and John and Dean managed to get the extra $100,000 without me.

We doubled sales again the next year, closing 2003 with four million dollars in sales. That was a long way from the projections in the business plan, but to be fair, we hadn't raised the cash required to meet those projections, which were based on raising five million. Percentage wise we were very close, but there was a window of opportunity and a market penetration factor that the extra money would have given us, meaning a compounding effect on sales due to branding alone.

By the time we launched our plan room, we were hard at work adding "on the fly" pricing, tracking, reports, address book functionality, and tons of internal software that clearly made us the best in the industry, but we lacked the horsepower to get the message out.

A roll-up of the reprographic industry was taking place, and new competitors were coming to market. A roll-up is when investors buy up a lot of regional or mom and pop companies and put them all under one corporate umbrella. This could be good or it could be bad depending on which side you're on. However, coming into the summer of 2004 we could see that we would finish the year with over seven million dollars in sales with no additional staff. Dean seemed pleased, but as he said in a board meeting, he wasn't getting any younger, and although we had done well with such a small cash infusion, just think what we could do if we raised five million dollars in a series B. This would represent our 2nd round of financing. Each financing round is referred to as a "Series".

We now had proof of concept and I fired John G from the board. Dean had a friend, Jim M, who had just become available and who would work as our CFO. Dean felt confident that Jim M could raise the money. I agreed to it as long as Bart and I could get a pay raise with full board approval. We had taken very modest salaries these last four years and I felt we deserved it.

Jim M came on as our CFO in 2004, and together we wrote the business plan and acquired two term sheets within a couple of months after bringing him on. Both of the term sheets were for five million dollars with scaled performance valuations that began at seven million pre money but could go to ten million based on hitting some of the projections.

Those were decent term sheets, and I felt sure that we could get a great deal from one of the two venture capital companies. One was local and known for being "Southern gentlemen," and the other was from North Carolina and was fairly new with their first fund. Neither had ever worked together before. I got non-disclosure agreements (NDAs) from both companies, which meant they couldn't discuss the information with anyone outside their organization. (I will not mention the names of the VC's and will use different names were needed from here on out due to what was to come) I liked the valuation methodology of the local group but liked the terms for liquidation preference, redemption privilege, and board seats of the East Coast company. I decided to blend the best terms of the two and get a deal that wasn't great but would be fair considering the times we were in, which was that there had not been any IPO activity in years, and that is where most VCs get their return, or so I thought. For those of you that don't know, an IPO is an Initial Public Offering, which is putting your stock for sale to the public and being listed on the public exchanges.

Then I made my first mistake. I told the local VCs that I wanted to work with them because of their reputation, experience, and proximity, but that I would like to see the liquidation preference lowered and the redemption privilege extended. I didn't push for more than that, and that wasn't the mistake. Where I messed up was when I told them I was asking for that because I had another term sheet that I wasn't going to ask them to match, just to tweak theirs a bit to get close. They were the ones I wanted to work with. They said to give them a day or two to think about it and they would get back to me.

Later in the week, I called to see if they were going to send a new term sheet and they said yes, it would be on my desk in the morning. To my surprise it was a joint term sheet from the two companies for a total of five million dollars with all the tougher terms of the local firm. I no longer had two term sheets; I had one with the two competing firms now partners.

By that time, I was fairly accustomed to having that sort of thing happen to me. I had been through a number of lawsuits with employees over stolen customer lists, broken deals with business partners, and general dishonesty, but this was pretty blatant. They had violated the non-disclosure agreements. One of the VC partners who ran the deal for the local firm would tell me later over wine that the second I told his partner that I had another term sheet, he was put to work calling every VC firm in the region asking if they were looking at PEI until he found my East Coast firm. The conversation then went something like, "Why don't the two of us split the risk and both get a better deal together?" Sad, but this is one of the first things one should know when dealing with VCs.

I made a few quick phone calls to some firms Jim had not gone to and shipped plans to two firms overnight. One was in New York and one in Phoenix. I had a deadline on the term sheet from the new combo VC, and the feedback from the new companies was that they might be able to do better on the pieces that were a problem for me, but they would need more time. I did not want to lose a bird in the hand, and Jim M said he thought it was the best we could do, plus he had a good feeling about the local firm.

Evil in the Boardroom

We closed the round in December 2004, with the condition that John's shares (the COO) would be wiped out or drastically reduced to be in line with what was normal. It was either that or I would have to suffer the full dilution of his shares from my percentage. Jim M contacted John to let him know he was getting a reduction in his shares because Jim had studied our corporate by-laws and the amount that was supposed to be given actually disagreed or was not in compliance with the bylaws and the option language that John himself had helped write when he did the by-laws and stock option plan. In John's efforts to limit options he forgot to take himself and his option agreement into consideration. John was very upset and threatened to sue, but it was quickly taken care of with a settlement. The other condition was that I would hire a new COO and a VP of sales.

13

Plan Express – The Bad

Plan Express was now funded with what we believed would be all the money we would ever need for the success we knew we could achieve. However, I was about to learn again the hard way how venture capital really works.

To be successful with venture capitalists, you either need to have an extremely strong proposition that makes them want you more than you want them or you need to be aware of their mind set and be ok with it. VCs have some "VC 101" principles they are engrained with and they rarely vary from them. This is the first thing you need to know.

I had already been weakened by the breaking of the NDA confidentiality agreement by my two VCs but I wouldn't realize the effects of that for four years. As 2005 began, we were to hire the COO and sales VP. This kicked off the second thing you need to know about VC rules which is that: This is the time to spend all of the money you raised, and they will put the people in place to do just that. If they can get you to burn through the cash fast, it will force you to do another round of capital raising. Then there is a lot to lose for the founder and a lot to gain for the VC.

Evil in the Boardroom

When you receive that much money—five million dollars—seemingly way more than needed, you cannot imagine blowing through it but the spending starts on day number one. First you receive the bills from the investors' due diligence, which includes expensive accountants, lawyers, and technology experts. Next you get the bill for the VC's legal team to do the closing documents plus, of course, your get your own attorney's bill. Then there is the up-front retainer for the executive recruiter that the VC insists you use, plus the marketing consultant who will be brought in to assist with a marketing plan and strategy. That's $500,000 gone, and nothing has happened yet.

We interviewed five candidates for COO and four for the VP of sales. Say good-bye to another $50,000 in expenses for their travel. We hired the COO, who negotiated with the VC directly (they ran the compensation committee for the board) and spent in excess of $100,000 to compensate for his country club losses, home sale, and moving expense. The COO then purchased a new accounting software package for $700,000, a new phone system and software for $450,000, and new servers and equipment for over one million dollars.

The VP of sales hired ten salespeople with very high base salaries that would exceed one million dollars our first year. At the end of the day, only two of those hires produced any sales. The trade show budget was doubled with T-shirt giveaways and pointless marketing materials. Next was $480,000 for fail over protection for our servers, which we had just put in place at a cost of $390,000 as part of the one million just mentioned. Then four more software developers were hired, at $100,000 each who produced nothing after a one-year period and had to be let go. Then we incurred $560,000 in outsourcing costs to do the work they were supposed to do. By the end of the first year, the money was essentially gone even with the addition of two million dollars in sales from me and the existing team.

The next year we added three million in sales due to the new hires, but then the old team quit over the new compensation plan.

Toward the end of 2005, Jim M could see the writing on the wall. He told me that it was obvious that the VC wanted all the money gone quickly and would destroy us in a "C" round.

Jim M had reached out to the large company doing the roll-up and had initial talks that led him to believe they were interested in acquiring us. Jim M was confident that we could get a valuation based on three times current sales. That is what the large companies stock was then trading at, and we were a fast-growing company. Most of the repro shops being bought were in decline. We were an anomaly.

Jim negotiated a talking points deal with the company and in early 2006, he made a presentation at the board meeting; the firm would buy us for thirty to thirty-five million dollars. That was based on a conservative estimate of 2006 sales of eleven million. It was the first time I had seen the lead partner from the local VC lose his cool. He yelled at Jim and I and said there was no way they were in it for a quick flip, and that the company was going to be worth more than one hundred million. He stormed out and that was that. I received a phone call from Dean an hour later as he was leaving from the Memphis airport. He told me that I had to fire Jim. I said I would not fire Jim. Dean said the board had the votes and there was no sense going to war over it. He assured me he could help Jim find something else. Again, I felt I had no choice. So I fired him. That was very hard for me to do. Jim was a friend and had done a great job. His mistake was that he went against the VCs plans.

14

Plan Express – The Ugly

2006 was a year of maneuvering by the COO for my position. You see, the next rule in the VC handbook is to fire the founder. My COO had weekly private meetings with the VC and was in constant direct communication via e-mail and phone. He was their man and he would do whatever he was told. He also had a very nice stock option grant that was given to him at his hiring by the VC.

We finished the year with sales in excess of eleven million dollars and had finished our placement of strategic print locations to lower our shipping costs and capture local business. We added a new location whenever the cost savings of shipping from that location would pay for the overhead of that office. This was a way to rapidly expand the company for virtually no money. We had started doing this prior to the Series B and the funded business plan was based on that premise. Putting a sales person at each location got us the local penetration. We needed that as we were rapidly becoming the national market leader in remote print and ship and this would give us the additional avenues and market segment to grow beyond that.

We also began work on a secret project. In the construction industry, when a General Contractor has a job, they put it out to sub-contractors to bid on. This process involves a lot of documents going back and forth and there can be a lot of legal issues that arise in regards to what information was received and when. At that time, there was no software in the marketplace to manage this, so I saw an opportunity to develop an invitation to bid system. However, I had been made aware of e-mails that some of the board members had passed around speaking about "Dewayne's crazy ideas." So we undertook this project in secret, keeping it even from the COO and luckily it was launched in 2007.. Without it we would have been toast. That is how fast the landscape was changing.

We ran very short of cash at the beginning of 2007 because the COO bought print machines based on his projections rather than actual sales. We now had seventeen machines when we should have had only twelve at the beginning of the year and fourteen at the end. That was about four machines too many during the year. They were $150,000 apiece, and the maintenance was around $10,000 per month for the extra machines. That mistake required a quick loan from the VCs of $400,000 under the same valuation terms as the original financing, even though we were doing twice the sales. Our valuation was essentially the same now as a 12 million dollar in sales company as it was when the company was doing just 4 million in sales. Hardly fair but they are holding all the cards.

About that same time, they negotiated a line of credit for one million dollars with covenants tied to performance. That money was quickly dumped into the cash flow stream, and I knew we were in big trouble.

In May of that year, I found out our COO was holding back shipments from customers to avoid paying overtime or giving the FedEx drivers donuts or twenty bucks to extend our deadline in an emergency. We lost two significant accounts because of it. We were on pace to do sixteen million dollars in sales that year, and it was coming undone with his lack of customer care.

One of his practices was to monitor how long it took for a customer to hang up in frustration and then calculate how long to leave them on hold to keep the customer service costs down. I started to come down pretty hard on him when he lied to me about those things and the fact that he was meeting in secret with the VC. I then found out that he had applied for a position with another company and flew there on our dime. That allowed me to fire him. The board was not happy, but there was nothing they could do, he had messed up.

Bart and I took over to fix things. Production was a disaster, and it turned out to be worse than I had imagined. We had lost a number of customers due to production issues. We finished the year with fourteen million dollars in sales, less than the projections but we had fixed the production issues with a lot of hard work. In addition, for the first time, we had started turning monthly profits.

I invited the board to a meeting in Arizona in September 2007 to celebrate our saving of the production process, the return of lost customers, and finally being profitable. I let them know that I was comfortable running operations and sales. I had hired an operations manager I had met a few years earlier, and he was giving us all the reports we required to run efficiently. We had righted the sinking ship.

Our agreement with the VC included a five year redemption privilege timeline – I'll explain more about that in a bit. The

Evil in the Boardroom

quick explanation is that I had that much time to get the company to at least twenty-five million dollars in sales. If I didn't reach that goal, I could be wiped out and left with nothing by the VC exercising the right to sell the company and invoking their liquidation preference. We only had 2 years left on the redemption privilege timeline. Once again I was in for a shock based on the comments at the meeting. There were words of praise and congratulations followed by, "Now we can afford to hire a big-time CEO." Huh?

They very carefully explained to me, the numbskull, that a CEO was necessary to take the company over the top. They had many examples of companies where the founder had stepped aside to let a high-profile CEO take a company to new heights. I said that I would be nervous that he might fire me, and what protection would I have if that occurred?

The lead VC explained that they would write a very lucrative severance plan for me that would last past the redemption period, and of course, I would always have my stock. The back and forth went on and on. I still had the numbers if it went to a board vote if Dean voted with me, so I was inclined to keep fighting, that was until the browbeating turned into more of a demand. I guess they call it bullying now.

I agreed to explore the option of hiring a CEO and said I would hire the perfect candidate if we could find one. Looking at the situation we were in with the recession begining, I decided that it was unlikely that either I or anyone else was going to get enough sales in the time remaining to avoid me getting wiped out. When I pointed that out, I was assured over and over that they would never sell the company

79

until it was time. They also stressed that I should choose the best course of action for success, which was hiring a superstar CEO.

Many business founders I have talked to do not understand what redemption privilege is. The easiest explanation is that if you sign a deal that has a five-year redemption privilege clause, the VC have the right to sell (redeem) their stock at that time. In addition, they have Liquidation Preference, meaning they get paid a multiple on the original investment in addition to the preferred stock. My deal called for 2x Liquidation Preference. What this means is that with the preferred stock, when sold, they also get back two times liquidation preference plus the accumulated dividends owed by the company. To recap, they receive two times the five million first for the liquidation preference, which equals ten million, then the preferred stock sale for five million, the amount they put in. Now you must pay the 8 percent accumulated dividend for the five years, for two million dollars. That totals seventeen million dollars, and they can exercise all this at the 5 year Redemption Privilege timeline.

That does not count the loans and certainly not a "C" round. Even if the company was doing twenty-five million in sales with the series "A" pay off of another two million, the existing loans outstanding would take another two to three million dollars. Total due as it stood was over twenty million dollars. Even if we sold the company for one times sales, or twenty-five million, which would be an appropriate price at the time, the remaining four million or so would be split according to ownership percentage. As I was now at approximately 30 percent, I would get under a third of the remaining four million dollars—right around one million if everything went well. The problem was that the VCs might decide to sell the company for twenty million or less and the common stock would be worth zero. There was no incentive for them to hold out for a higher price once they were got their target met, so the likelihood of my receiving any money from a forced sale was also zero.

Of course, if at the five year mark, the VCs decided to not sell the company because we were on a roll or there were no buyers, it would benefit me dramatically. A delayed redemption timeline would allow for the company to grow and increase my chances of a big payoff (i.e. if the company were worth more, I would be paid more once the 20 plus million of locked in obligations were met). For that reason and because I had significant doubt that we could hit the numbers I agreed to search for a new CEO, but only if he could raise a "C" round to launch and fund another secret project, the project lead and public bid solicitation software, that we were calling eBidroom. As an incentive to get me to do that, the VCs said they would provide a loan of $300,000 to finance the CEO search under the same terms as the "B" round and give me the severance plan referenced earlier.

To digress slightly for those considering raising venture capital and to make it clearer, consider the following. With a five-year redemption privilege in place, the VCs have the right to sell their stock at that time—either back to you or, if you can't afford it (and you can't), to sell the company to exit. In that scenario the VCs would now be due seventeen million dollars on the five million they put into the company (you would not receive any of the money). With those very standard terms, the real interest rate on the deal is around 75 percent per year! If you point that out to the VCs, they will reassure you that it is not a problem. They will add a clause that states that if you go public or liquidate the company, as long as their minimum payout is twenty-five million, the two times preference goes away.

It will then be pointed out to you that if you believe in your plan, which surely you must, why would you not believe in giving them a fivefold return on their investment. You must believe your company is worth more than that, so what's the big deal? Almost all deals work this way. They get huge returns no matter what happens unless the company tanks. Even then, they will still most likely recoup the original investment in the liquidation.

The only way a VC deal works for a founder is if the company soars, the economic conditions are very good, the M&A market is active and the company still has huge market share to capture. I am sure you are very confident in your plan, but 90 percent of the time, your projections will not meet your expectations.

We closed 2007 with over fourteen million dollars in sales, as stated earlier. I was deep into the CEO search and looking for the superstar. I had met with Dean, and it was his opinion that I would not find Mr. Right because I was the guy. With a background in numerous start-ups, management of companies of up to one hundred million dollars, a thorough knowledge of reprographics and technology, expertise in the construction industry, and a proven record in sales, there was no one who could do better with the company. I thanked him for that and kept it in the back of my mind while interviewing the candidates and working my butt off to grow sales and keep the company profitable.

Not only was I going through this intense change and pressure with my business, but at the same time, I also experienced some devastating personal losses. Remember when my mother had begun behaving strangely and I attributed it to stress? Well it was the beginning of Alzheimer's and she eventually passed away from it. We also lost Debbie's dad Al, and our beloved golden retriever Cody, who was only seven years old, all within this two year period

15

Plan Express – The Very Ugly

In February 2008 we rolled out our budget for a conservative sales number of eighteen million dollars for year end. The board wanted much more, but I would not bend that time. I had learned that they liked to push our top-line sales forecast so they could increase the overhead and sales budget associated with it and that would in turn ensure we would need more money from them. I refused, even though we were already ahead on the sales forecast. It was also the first time I met Jack.

We had actually made an offer of employment to a guy who was very likeable and smart and had a great reputation as a CEO for hire for a large private equity firm. He had managed five companies in ten years for them and said he was interested. We made him an offer, but it was countered by his employer when he gave notice. The next candidate, Jack, arrived from Atlanta and spent the morning with Bob, the junior partner, and the late afternoon with John, the senior VC. I was to meet him for dinner at the Madison Grille in downtown Memphis.

Jack's demeanor was very relaxed and jovial at first blush. He was well spoken and seemed to take great pride in the fact that he had graduated from an Ivy League school. He had an Irish father who was a firefighter, a loving family, came from a sports background, and had a success story to tell.

His story was that of a technology guy out of college with an entrepreneurial spirit. He founded a technology company, got VC funding, and got screwed by the VC. He went on to work for an owner of a trucking firm and took the company from 15 million to 120 million dollars in sales.

He boasted that one of his greatest talents was the ability to protect the owner from the investor. He said he had a unique way of communicating with investors and giving them the information they wanted to see without compromising the founder's vision. He claimed he was the guy who would do exactly what I wanted him to do while still making the VC happy, because really, all they wanted was a fancy presentation and someone who could talk the talk. He was my guy; I could trust him. He said he would relocate to Memphis. Those were his words. Wow, maybe I had found our superstar.

I called the senior partner and the recruiter in the morning and said we could move forward with references and the psychology test. We used a firm to administer a test that would show intelligence, decision-making skills, social skills, and a stress analysis. The test was done within a day or two, and we had the results within the week. The results were positive except for "under stressful situations." The doctor's statement said that Jack was likely to make serious errors in judgment if angry or in a stressful situation. I called the senior VC and told him that, as much as I liked the guy, the results were troubling. He agreed with me but assured me he would step in and be mindful of the analysis and make sure things never got out of hand. I asked if the recruiter had gotten back to him with references yet, and he said no, but he would proceed with an offer pending the references.

A couple days later, I was informed that an offer had been made but there was some kickback on the relocation package. Again I asked for the references; still no reply, so I called the recruiter myself. He said that he had conducted them himself and everything was positive. I would have the notes in a few minutes. I received the spreadsheet with notes from three references and was greatly concerned because all three had worked for him at his former 120-million-dollar success story and with him on a start-up he was in the process of liquidating.

I called the recruiter back and asked if we could interview an employer versus a fellow employee, and he blew me off in a huff. When I called the senior VC to share my frustration, he informed me that Jack had accepted the position and would commute for three or four months and then relocate. He said references didn't matter at that point and that the recruiter had done his job, so I was to make sure he got paid.

Red flags were flying, but the deal was done. Jack was starting the following Monday. I found out in the next week that two of the references he provided would be hired immediately and the third brought on as a consultant. We had no need for any employees in any of those positions or capacities.

Jack's first week in March was a big love fest. He wanted to meet everyone and let him or her know that he was the CEO now but Dewayne was not going anywhere and we were going to do great things. He would spend the next few months learning the business and then use his experience and knowledge to put mechanisms in place for higher sales and greater profits. He would also write a first-class investment-grade business plan for a "C" round of three million dollars. His second week was spent interviewing the controller and introducing his technology friend and CFO friend (his references) as his new hires to the appropriate teams.

Jack and his tech guy, Morton, had flown in on Monday in Morton's plane with another programmer. They left on Wednesday because there was a storm coming. That became a pattern for a while until I started to take issue with it. Jack then started flying on Delta, arriving early afternoon on Mondays and leaving on Thursday or Friday mornings.

In April Jack made it clear he wanted to go visit the sales team, specifically the number one salesperson, Erin, in Arizona, and a girl we just hired named Kristin in Dallas. He would call all ten of them and introduce himself first.

The first call went out to Monique. Jack left her a message to call him back. He waited two hours and called her again. When she answered, Jack asked her why she didn't call him right back, as he was the CEO, which she should know from the company memo. She said she knew but that she was working on a demo with a client. Jack let her know that she was to return his calls immediately. Monique told him she thought he was being rude. Jack responded that he wanted her to think overnight about what she had done. She said she would do that and get back to him the next morning.

He shared that story with me right after it happened, and I noticed he was sweating and shaky. He said he was an inch away from firing her on the spot. I tried to calm him down and let him know that I was sure he just took it the wrong way. I then called Monique on the way home and asked her to please call in the morning and just say it was a misunderstanding and that she would return his call right away next time. She let me know that she didn't think she could do it. She was very upset. I received her resignation in the morning.

Next on deck was Kristin, who was coming to Memphis for a week of training. On her first night in town, my assistant and I took her out for a welcome dinner and introduction, and I went home afterward. Kristin called me a couple of hours later. Her comment was that she had really screwed up and was probably getting fired. I didn't know what she was talking about. She told me she had gone out alone after dinner and ran into Jack and had drinks with him. He walked her back to the hotel and took her to her room. She claimed he was being very suggestive but she got him to go away.

She then said her cell phone rang and she thought it was me, so the first words out of her mouth were, "Jack is such a douche bag," at which point there was silence and she then realized it was him. Why she thought it was me, I have no idea. The whole story made no sense whatsoever, and I still don't understand what really happened, but the situation was not good.

The reason for telling this story is that his bizarre behavior became the norm. Every week there was a new story from another person about weird behavior in downtown Memphis. My controller came into my office on day upset because one of her girlfriends had told her that she was considering dating the new single CEO at Plan Express. The problem for her was that she knew he was already with one of her other girlfriends.

It appeared that Jack was trying to date two different women at the same time but the reality was that he married with two small children at home.

Jack stayed at the Peabody Hotel and every night, he had expensive dinners with guests. These were all charged to his expense account. When reconciling his expenses he demanded a wire the day he turned them in. When asked for receipts he told the controller to do the wire transfer and not to worry about the receipts. Jack put in a wire request for Morton for a couple thousand dollars, and when asked for an invoice or documentation, the controller was told to do as she was told. She quit the next day. Amy had been with me for seven years. Her replacement lasted three weeks, but not before filing a damning resignation letter saying she had never seen such a lack of controls and standards in her life. That letter was swept under the rug by the board.

I was not made aware of those events until after Amy was gone. Also during that time, I gave Jack a secondary American Express Black Card. He had seen it when I paid for our dinner during the interview. He asked how I got the card, and I let him know that I used the card to pay our FedEx bills. It gave us another thirty days on our cash flow needs plus an additional 4-percent discount from FedEx. It also got me to the threshold required to qualify for the card. I had to personally guarantee payment on the card, which was never an issue, and in return for the guarantee, I got the points. He knew the perks the card provided and said that having a card would be a great incentive for him. I had agreed at the dinner, and he now had it.

I took a long weekend vacation on May 16, 2008, and while driving received a phone call from Jack and Gil, the production manager.

Evil in the Boardroom

They were calling to inform me that they had closed the Nashville office that morning. Jack said the closing was going to save the company $400,000 per year.

Stunned, my question to him was, where did he get his numbers to make the decision? He said he got them from Amy before she quit. Amy understood our business finances as well as anyone, after all she had been the controller for seven years. I called her later, and she said he never asked and she never gave him any numbers.

While on the phone call, I let both Jack and Gil know that we saved over two dollars on every package that shipped from Nashville to the Southeast and that Nashville averaged 120 packages a day. Closing the Nashville office would cost us over $5,000 per month in extra shipping cost, plus we were doing almost $400,000 per year in local printing business in Nashville that we would lose. We only had three employees there, with a total overhead of less than $200,000. We also had a lease for $2,800 per month for the next year that we couldn't get out of.

What was I missing?

His response when confronted with the facts was, "Hey, they need their pound of flesh." The supposed savings cost us a fortune and only set the stage for more to come. I really did not understand at the time or at least give enough push back on one of the board members desire to reduce our footprint. He would bring it up at board meetings but I thought he understood the cost savings and marketing advantage of having the remote locations. I mean after all, he came from GE management training. Apparently his message was clear in Jack's mind.

16

Plan Express – The Stupid

I received a note from one of my board members in June that it was the board's intention to close all of our satellite locations. We had eight locations total.

One of the core principles of the original business plan, which the VC had invested in, was for us to open a print location in an area as soon as the shipping volumes to that area provided a large enough zone shipping discount to pay for the associated overhead of the individual location. The cost of printing in one place versus another was the same as long as the volume was sufficient, which it would have to be, based on the number of packages shipping from that location.

Once in that location, with at a minimum break-even status, a salesperson could be stationed in that office and establish a local presence. That enabled us to attract customers such as contractors who only did work locally and otherwise would have no use for our print and ship service.

When the VC "experts" were looking at our fixed cost problem, which consisted mostly of equipment leases, they did not take into consideration the fact that the terminated COO had gotten way ahead of the curve with the purchase of four machines we didn't need. If they were to close down the seven remaining locations, we would lose much of our business and destroy the ability to grow sales. We would also lose a huge profit margin on the shipping, as everything would now be charged to us at zone 5 rates. (We would charge our customers a flat rate and profited from the proximity rates.)

We had a high market penetration in the print and ship sector and were barely scratching the surface of the local print provider sector. Our offices were paid for and, due to our shipping volume, were never below breakeven. I pointed that out a number of times, but the academics had made a decision and were not about to take advice from me.

Jack was trying to work on the new business plan and the eBid-room concept for the "C" round and wasn't getting anywhere. He asked me for a copy of what we had done for the "B" round, and I went over it with him but let him know that no one would invest in the current plan of print and ship. That ship had sailed.

He would need to revise the entire model to become more like that of a content provider via our eBidroom idea and charge either by the file or via subscription for the digital downloads to the sub-contractor. In my series "A" business plan and the series "B" business plan, which I had made a focal point, was my theory of a paradigm shift that would take place at some point in the next few years. That shift was defined as "the end user or purchaser of the product will no longer be the General Contractor (the GC), but the sub-contractor (the sub)." That would have great significance because the GCs had commoditized the repro industry due to their large purchases and buying power. Subcontractors did not have that leverage and never would, and they were currently paying five to ten times more for the same set of blueprints. The eBidroom model exploited that.

Trying to explain that concept was extremely frustrating, and it fell on deaf ears. Jack knew he had to make a case for eBidroom, even though he didn't understand it, but it was all he had left. He came to me after a week and asked if he could use a friend in Atlanta to finish the plan because he had writer's block. I agreed that we needed to move forward quickly, and his friend took over. He turned out to be Jack's third reference.

17

Plan Express – Put a fork in it; it's done. The Ivy League Clown. Another Surprise.

In June 2008, Jack fired Woodie. Woodie was my first executive hire back in 2000 and was also a board member of the International Reprographics Association. Woodie was widely respected in the industry and served as not only our ambassador to the industry but also managed our largest account, Johnson & Johnson and their overseas operations. Woodie had some health issues that took a while to resolve, and I knew that Jack had a problem with that. He also did not like having a high-level employee in place who was loyal to me. Woodie thought he got fired because he had walked in on Jack while Jack was watching porn on his work computer.

That firing was another fatal mistake. I called the senior VC and told him I had real concerns with our new CEO's character and work ethic. Also, he was not meeting his commitments for relocating, and I would like to discuss it all. His response to me was word for word: "Dewayne, you just need to get over the fact that you are no longer the CEO." That was the end of the conversation, and so much for the Southern gentleman routine. I would later get calls from two other former founders of firms invested in by the same venture capital company with similar stories.

In July 2008, we were running low on cash. Our profits ended in April, and Jack's spending was dragging us down, so was the cost and loss of revenue from the closing of remote locations, with Dallas being next.

I received a call from American Express saying I needed to send a check for $290,000 and that my card was on hold. There was a $400,000 outstanding balance on the card. I immediately called Jack and let him know that I was personally responsible for the card and he needed to pay it. He told me he had made an executive decision and used the money for more important things. I told him that was unacceptable, and he told me he would not be bullied by me. Jack was also in the process of arranging to move our server farm to Atlanta as part of the restructuring and proceeding with closing San Francisco, then Phoenix, then New York, and then Chicago. I seriously felt as though I was in The Twilight Zone.

In August, the eBidroom business plan was returned, and Jack presented it to the board. I had seen a preview of it and knew then that the intent was to not really make an effort to raise money from a source other than our local VC. To describe the plan as "amateurish" would be a supreme compliment. Dean saw it and said it was an embarrassment. The local VC didn't think it was so bad and volunteered to provide the series "C" funding of three million dollars plus rolling in the loans at a seven- million-dollar valuation and limiting their antidilution privileges. (That was another clause in the deal prior.) Under that clause the full dilution of shares would come from the series "A" and my own shares only.

Evil in the Boardroom

That would leave me with less than 10 percent of the company and no chance for any payoff, as the break even mark for me to realize any money was now probably over thirty million with this deal. I asked for a chance to redo the plan and see if I could get a better deal somewhere else. How could I accept a valuation at one half of current sales? It made no sense at all. The VCs said sure, go for it.

Three weeks later I returned with a term sheet for ten million dollars at a thirty-million-dollar valuation based on the eBidroom model, combined with the paradigm shift I still believed would happen. The valuation was twenty-one million dollars better, or four times higher. As you might imagine, I was quite pleased with my efforts and let the board know that I had a term sheet to share. I had made the mistake of sharing the information with Jack prior to the meeting. Our junior and senior VCs made a mockery of the term sheet and said they would refuse "stupid" money that added no value other than cash.

The structure of the board was seven members. Two were my appointees, so including myself, I had three votes; they had three votes because Jack had a board seat at that point, and Dean would be the tie breaker. If he abstained, we would then go to a shareholder vote, which I would lose because the loans given by the series "B" VCs now brought their shares just under mine, so the series "A" votes would be the deciding factor and I already knew they would not be in my favor. A fight of that caliber would destroy the board and the company, which I was willing to do, except that we were so upside down on payables. The phone lines and Internet service were starting to be cut off, and of course there was the Amex card and a few suppliers, including our paper supplier, who had given us notice. I also knew that all the covenants had been broken on the bank line of credit. We had one week to do the due diligence for the new VC and get the money and it would be next to impossible to do. That along with the fact that they would also see the idiotic business decisions being made, and probably run for hills, left me with no choice and I never brought it to a vote.

We closed on the series "C" in September with the existing VC, which I signed under protest. The money was brought in, and I asked as chairman of the board for a full accounting of how it was going to be spent. The money was to provide for the rollout of eBidroom, improving the notification system, building the sub-contractor database, and acquiring more construction content along with overall marketing.

We had another board meeting in December, and I asked where we were money wise and was told I would be given a spreadsheet. I never received it. I asked repeatedly and was ignored.

I spent the rest of 2008 working on sales and was successful in cutting six salespeople from the team and maintaining sales of over fourteen million dollars in spite of the shop closing. Now we were about as big as we could get with the business model of having just one central facility. Far short of projections but good considering.

I had mentioned during a meeting that, for the first time in the history of the company, our July sales were less than June's. We have always been a leading indicator of economic conditions, being so closely tied to retail. The recession was steepening. My hope at the time was that people claiming to know a lot more than me about economics were making the right decisions and that everything would all work out. They all predicted a 12 to 14 month recession.

As we entered 2009, fewer than nine months since Jack was hired, the reports of reckless and absurd behavior continued. Jack traveled to San Francisco to assist in the closing, and I was told that he showed up blind drunk. We had negotiated high-end office furniture into the lease, since the owner of the building was in the furniture business. When Jack got there, rather than have the things moved or put in storage or even resold or returned to the landlord in exchange for the lease payments due, he instructed the staff to throw them all in the Dumpster.

I found out from the accounting department that Jack had made a deal with Océ, our printing equipment supplier, to take back all machines that were still in the lease period for a charge of $660,000. When those machines were purchased, we had a choice of a full market value lease or a one-dollar buy. Every machine we had was done as a one-dollar buy. That meant that they had a positive residual value at about the three-year mark. Many of the machines turned in had twenty-five to fifty thousand dollars of positive equity value. Some were a push and two were negative. Overall I would say slightly positive, but a break-even at worst. There was no way we should have written a check for $660,000.

My assistant during that entire time was one of my most trusted employees. I gave her access to everything I did and any and all information. I knew she would keep me informed and had my back.. She also became Jack's assistant and picked him up from the airport, worked with him all day, and acted as his secretary.

She called to tell me that Jack had a severe drinking problem. On one occasion she had to circle the airport a few times on a Thursday morning while he vomited out of her truck because he was still drunk. I had told him he was not allowed to use my Black Card anymore after he would not pay the Amex bill. I no longer let the company use it for FedEx either. It was my personal card with my personal guarantee and it was not to be used. Jack asked me to do him a personal favor and allow him to carry it because of the perks when flying. I agreed as long as he did not charge on it. He had finally paid off the balance with part of the "C" round proceeds.

In February 2009, Jack decided that we should try to sell our technology as a service to some of the content providers or the reprographic service industry. Our sales had dropped to levels of the year prior due to the recession and the shop closings. Jack was cutting staff aggressively, as if we were in shutdown mode. He was buying managers' contracts out with large bonuses. He was paying off leases for early exits.

At that point not one penny of cash or an ounce of effort had gone into eBidroom. Jack had no intention of relocating to Memphis and was now showing our back end technology to anyone who wanted to see it without a nondisclosure agreement. I asked my assistant if Morton ever signed an NDA and she said no. I then asked Jack to have him sign one, he had access to everything and Jack was going forward with moving the server room to Atlanta. His comment was, "I don't need him to sign anything."

Jack actually got a bite from Reed Construction Data on using our invitation to bid technology on a subscription basis. Jack then overpriced it enough to solve all of our problems. It was rejected, and Reed moved on.

In late February, Jack called an emergency meeting in Memphis and wanted input from the sales team, which now consisted of two people plus me. Jack brought us into the conference room and informed us that, to survive, we had to make a fundamental change in the way the business pricing model was structured. He had come to the conclusion that GCs were no longer buying as much paper and that subs were open to taking digital downloads and printing the plans themselves, or using an online takeoff tool. The recession had accelerated the timeline for the paradigm shift I had predicted; it was happening, and we were ill prepared, because no money had gone into eBidroom.

Jack's answer to the situation was that we needed to charge our customers on the upload of their files into the plan room as a means to support free downloads to the subs. Our current policy was that two sets of plans must be ordered or paid for in order to have free downloads for the subs. Jack said the current method did not produce enough revenue and that we needed to charge the equivalent of four or maybe seven sets for us to cover our costs. He first suggested a $7 per file charge, and with massive amounts of arguing and debate, we got him down to $3.50 per file.

He informed us it was our job to sell the new pricing model to our current customers for our survival. We all agreed we would do it. I did ask if he planned on doing anything with eBidroom and he said no. He and Gil had made the decision that the combination of the shop closings, the upload charge, and selling our technology to reprographers was the answer. Erin and I agreed to attend the IRGA show in Pittsburgh to help Jack and Gil present his plan to the industry and to host a private party for reprographers. We would go from there to the SPECS show to meet with many of our customers firsthand to explain the new pricing model and to ensure acceptance.

The IRGA show was a bust. Erin and I staffed the booth alone. Gil came by, and when we asked where Jack was, he said that Jack had run into an old college buddy the night before and was in no shape to come out until late in the afternoon for the suite party.

Sharing my frustration with my assistant, she warned me that I was really going to be mad when I saw my Amex bill. Jack had been using it again, without my permission (again, that was my personal card). There were numerous charges on it, including a twelve-dollar drink with a one-hundred-dollar tip at 4:00 a.m., another large dinner party for several hundred dollars, plus the hotel we were staying in and the car he was currently renting. I told her I was calling Amex and removing him from my account.

We held our private party and had two or three people show up. We talked up the benefits of using our "Planroom Processing" technology. It seemed well received, but to no audience. We went to dinner at a restaurant nearby where I made a stupid mistake.

Jack had a habit of baiting people with his own stories of daring, stupidity, and conquests. That night he was talking about all of his gambling trips to Vegas and how he was always compensated at the Winn, and how a VP of sales tried to seduce him into her room, and so on. He asked me, "Hasn't that ever happened to you?"

I said no it had not, but (here comes the stupid part) one time in Vegas I had ordered a massage in my room. During the massage I fell asleep, and when I awoke, three hundred dollars was missing from my pants pocket, but for some reason, she didn't take all my money, because there were still four hundred left. Ha-ha, isn't it fun sharing stories? I never said when it had occurred; it could have been twenty years ago for all they knew. This story would later come back to haunt me..

Apparently, my so called trusted assistant and confidant must have called Jack shortly after I spoke with her about how angry I was that he was using my card. She told him that I had just cancelled his card, because when dinner ended, he grabbed the tab and pulled out the Black Card to pay for it. Number one, it was my card, which he did not have permission to use; number two, it was an obvious FU. I grabbed the tab and handed the waiter my card.

Erin and I went to the SPECS convention and explained to dozens of customers what the new pricing change was, why it had been done, and how great it would be in the long run for their companies. It would save them on shipping and printing costs and cost less as a whole. It was well received at the time. It was the first weekend of March 2009.

I had told my wife, Debbie, earlier, around the first of the year, that she should prepare for a disaster. It was March, and I knew things were going to blow up. I warned her again that it might soon be over. I knew she did not believe me at the time, but realization was about to set in.

My phone started to ring immediately after our customers received the new billing. They explained that while they understood the situation and knew it would get better with a rebate for the printing program, it just wouldn't work, and they were no longer going to do business with Plan Express. I sent a letter about a week later to the entire board and let them know that six of our top ten accounts had left us and we were in serious trouble. On top of that, Jack's last chance at the repro technology service market evaporated when Service Point, who had shown a previous interest, walked away.

I arrived for the board meeting that followed in April to discuss what needed to be done. I was fairly confident I could get back the customers who had left if we quickly went back to the old pricing model. That would give us the time and money to adapt to the shift and weather the recession. I had also hoped there was still some of the round "C" money left for me to execute on the eBidroom plan, which would do very well with the paradigm shift in full tilt.

At that point, I knew that the VCs would not sell the company because it wasn't worth anything until the ship was righted once again, or at least stabilized. The redemption time deadline was only seven months away. My hope was that the VCs would wake up, consider extending the timeline, fire the CEO, and allow me to fix the company once again.

The meeting started with Dean asking about my e-mail regarding the six large customers who had left. In an overly dramatic display,

Evil in the Boardroom

Jack picked up a stack of accounting reports and screamed that he was tired of my lies to the board. "Here, right here, are reports that show every single customer Dewayne says is gone, placing orders. Dewayne, give me a name!"

I did, and he said, "Here is an order from them last night, give me another," and "OK, how about so and so? Here is an order from them from two days ago." Jack proclaimed he was tired of my interference and that here was a perfect example. He said every single customer in our top ten was still ordering and this was the proof. It was obvious he had prepared for the meeting, and I knew he was dead wrong, but at that point, Dean said, "Let's move on."

I had lost my will to fight that day. I knew, and Jack knew that the customers were gone; we had the daily sales reports. If that move was not a ploy and he really believed we had not lost customers, he was on something. The orders he was referencing were real, but what he didn't point out—and what I failed to recognize in the moment —was that those orders were downloads from our retailers' plan rooms being purchased by our GCs. Tiny sales of less than ten dollars in some cases instead of the normal thousand-dollar orders. They were not using us for their distribution at all; they were gone. He basically lied and got away with it while in the process making me look bad. I was defeated and didn't know what to do other than to keep working for a paycheck.

The next week Jack called me at home and said he had a proposal for me. Earlier in the year, he had said if we got to a certain point in the business that he called "red flag day," we should both stop drawing wages. He said we were at that point but he could not afford to do it and asked if I would be willing to take a six-month hiatus until he worked through things.

"After all, Dewayne, you own six million shares of stock and have that to protect, and I believe this is the best way for you to do it." He told me the board was tired of the fighting and I could continue to assist with sales but at no pay.

I pretended to act understanding and said to him that I needed a week to think it over and would get back to him. I was leaving in the morning for another important trade show and I would need some time. He said that was great and he really appreciated my help. On the inside I was furious. The man had destroyed my company, the VCs refused to see it, and he had thrown away the money with no plan for the future.

One week later I submitted my resignation as president and chairman of the board and put the company on notice that I would be bringing a lawsuit for breach of fiduciary duty, fraud, and embezzlement.

Within a couple of weeks, all of the key people in sales left the company. I asked Bart to stay. I knew that if he left the company it would sink immediately.

I then received a letter from Jack for "termination for cause" with a list of reasons. Number one was inappropriate conduct on company business (referring to my story of the massage). I was then accused of using my assistant to work on my personal business during working hours. They said this occurred when I asked her to replace the credit card stolen in said massage encounter. I was also accused of using the company credit card for personal gain (the points from my credit card), using a company credit card for personal reasons (an ancestry.com mistaken charge), being in possession of company property (?), and also obstruction and tortuous interference of the business. This last accusation was in reference to a voice mail that I left a coworker letting her know that I quit. Apparently they felt that I was trying to interfere with the business by doing that. None of that could have bothered me any more emotionally, I was already devastated, except for the accusation in regards to my assistant helping with replacing the stolen credit card.

I had asked her to put a hold on a lost credit card for me, one time when I was on a business trip in New York. I was in transit and in meetings and couldn't easily do it myself. It certainly had nothing to do with Vegas, a theft or a masseuse.

She had been my trusted confident and this really bothered me because it was such a blatant lie. Why was she deliberately trying to hurt me?

I decided to call her and I immediately asked her why she would say such a thing. She said because it was the truth. Obviously she was lying. Perhaps she had switched one instance for another to use against me for her own job protection. I let her know that the only time that she had ever worked to replace a card for me on company time was the time I thought I lost my card in New York the night prior to a full sales call day. I was at appointments the entire next day and I had asked her to call the restaurant where I used it last. I had the receipt and the phone number, but they didn't open until 11:00 a.m. and I'd be in meetings at that time. I had asked her to call and see if they had it and, if not, to place the card on hold and I would order a new one when I got home, since I would be in meetings all day and then had an early flight the next morning, I wanted to ensure that no one got a hold of it and used it.

I had returned to the hotel in New York at 6:00 p.m. that evening, and when I walked into the room with its freshly made bed, I could see the card underneath of it. It had fallen off the nightstand. I reminded her that I had called immediately to inform her of this, and she said she had cancelled the card and a new one was being sent and would be there by 8:30 a.m the next day. I reminded her that I had asked her why she would do that when all I wanted was a hold put on it, and she had replied that it was no big deal, there was not a charge. I then reminded her that I had a 9:00 a.m. flight so how could I be in a hotel room at 8:30am to receive the new credit card. She apologized and said she would rebook my flight, but I said never mind, I would take care of it. This was not just a single, simple phone call, it was a series of events that resulted in rescheduling of a flight from New York. How could she have forgotten that or mixed that up with the Vegas story?

After I recounted the episode to her that day on the phone, I said, "Do you remember that?" She said no, she had sent the card to Vegas.

I said, "Well, you need to find that FedEx number and the log from Amex, which I can easily get, to back up your claim, or you will be brought into it too, because I have the records for the entire history of the event. It was sent to New York and there was never a package to Vegas."

There was dead silence. I didn't know if it was because she was confused or duped or busted, or all of the above. I would never find out, but I let my board members know that they would lose that fight. I probably should have let it play out in hindsight, but I was very angry at the false charge they had concocted.

I next received phone calls from Erin and Kristin. They said that Jack had called them with the same type of baiting questions. "When you were traveling, did Dewayne ever do anything inappropriate or did you ever see him do anything inappropriate?" When they said no he kept pushing with more leading questions. He continued to push, but his questions went nowhere other than to prove how evil he was.

Letters went back and forth, and it was obvious they had no case for the termination, and I had a very good one against them, but it would be costly. I also had the problem of being on the board myself during the events, and even though I protested, I was in fact, by mere association, complicit in the eyes of the legal system. I would have to prove my objection at every move, and that would be difficult to document.

We were able to reach an agreement where I would be released from my employment agreement and terminated for no cause. I would receive a cash settlement, and each side would give the other a full release and hold harmless. Jack was out scrambling to dump the company. It was crashing fast and he couldn't hold it together.

He found a buyer in a competitor we will call the Y factor. The buyer agreed to purchase only the assets of the company and wanted a full release from me (which meant that I could never sue them in the future for anything). That was probably the largest reason for the settlement, but there was one catch. I would receive approximately one-third of my severance at the close and the balance eighteen months later. It was September 2009, sixteen years after starting the company and growing it to nearly seventeen million dollars in sales (annualized). I was walking away with very little except for the right to compete, I had a full release from my contract and a hold harmless. I would still own the six million shares of stock, but as they say, they were now worth less than the paper they were written on.

I had one problem that I wasn't sure how to deal with. During the negotiations I had made it known that Bart's livelihood was very important to me and a condition of the deal. PEI told me that the Y factor considered him a key if not the most important part of the purchase. That gave me a great deal of relief, and freed me up for my next venture. I decided to pursue an idea I had for a feature film project. I was going to make a movie.

I committed to making the movie with filming to begin October 1, 2009. The very same day Bart received his offer to work for Y factor. It was for fifty thousand less than he was making at PEI and he would have to relocate at his own expense immediately.

Bart called my old assistant for direction, she had been in charge of HR, but she would not return his calls. He let them know that the offer was not acceptable and continued working.

One week later, after not hearing from anyone despite numerous requests, he called Gil and was informed that he had in fact been terminated the week prior. He did not receive notice, his severance, his vacation pay, or anything. At that point Jack sent out a letter stating that he had been fired "for cause," the "cause" being that the company was sold. We would use that stupid letter as evidence that Bart did not have a non-compete, as his contract had been breached. Bart's severance was due unless he was fired for cause. Leave it to Jack to define "cause" as "be-cause the company was sold." Ivy League?

It was the substandard offer from Y factor and the unprofessional lack of response from my ex-assistant, as well as the icing on the cake—Jack's letter—that motivated me to start over with the birth of Pantera Global Technology.

18

Pantera Global Technology – Let the Lawsuits Begin

Bart and I had a very long talk the day he got his insulting offer from the new owner of Plan Express, renamed PENewco. His feelings were hurt. He had spent time with the Y factor team and had respect for those he dealt with. The whole ordeal had taken a toll on both of us.

It was early October 2009. I was fifty-five years old and had a fourteen-day production shoot for the movie I was starting. This would require eighteen hours a day of my time for the next two weeks. I would end up working on the movie edit for over a year and ultimately decide to not promote it as the cinematography and sound were substandard. I may reshoot it someday as I now have a very expensive demo that may be used to seek professional partners in the industry.

I was fairly sure I could get my old company, Lakeview Construction, to give us their work if we were to start a new company. This would give us a nice start, but we both agreed that, if we were going to do it again, it had to be something totally different from PEI. Had Bart been offered his old job and his old pay we wouldn't have started Pantera. I felt I still had something to prove, but I would not have gone into business competing against my son's employer. With Bart having no desire to move to Cincinnati, or to work for so much less pay, we decided to move forward.

The PEI model had not been allowed to follow the original business plan, nor had the investors listened to my instinct to adapt to the changes brought on by the recession or the fulfillment of the prediction of the paradigm shift. The recession had actually accelerated the shift, and we had the answer for it and could have prospered, but no one could see it in spite of my pleas.

While PEI was still in business as part of the Y factor, we believed there was an opportunity to take many of the PEI accounts. They would be forced to adapt to the changes required by the switch to the Y factor platform, giving us an opportunity to win them over.

We decided that the new company would be built in a modular fashion. It would be created to build community and cater to the subcontractor, taking full advantage of the shift. We would avoid building software that created little value, and we would come in at half the price of the cheapest provider in each category we entered.

I reached out to my old partner from Lakeview Construction who had bought out Gene. Kent and I had become very close friends in the years since I sold Lakeview. I let him know what had happened of late and asked if he would consider allowing my new company to provide our services to him. One of my previous employees, who had been terminated the same way Bart had, was already working for him. James had also been told he could stay on at half the pay and he would have to relocate. Kent let me know that it would not be a problem switching over as long as the service was as good and didn't cost more than he was currently paying.

I tasked Bart with finding a large-format printer and the other equipment we would need as well as getting a website built. Our back end would begin as nothing more than an FTP site that we bought for very little. We planned on replacing it with more of a plan room-type technology when we could.

I had set up a foreign corporation a few months earlier for a variety of reasons, from funding for the movie to asset protection, and also for protection from the unknowns that seemed to be hitting me from every direction. Our next step was to set up an Arizona LLC as a division of Pantera Global, our foreign corporation. A month or two earlier, I had posted a web page project on Crowdspring. com for a website design just in case I needed it. It came in handy for a quick start-up.

Bart spent the next three weeks getting set up in an office in Waukegan, Illinois, getting the printer, buying servers and office furniture, and arranging for data lines and phones. He had done the same for each of our seven remote locations at PEI, so it wasn't that big of a challenge for him. I would check in during the day for a minute or two, but making a movie as the executive producer is not an easy task. I also hired a bookkeeper to assist with all the corporate work and banking.

The stock market had just gone through a huge crash six months earlier, and my 401k, my IRA, and my personal stock accounts were all down 50 percent. The house had taken a hit of at least a million dollars. The only thing in my favor was my car collection. I had started to sell off stock out of various accounts a few years earlier and started buying classic cars. Although the market was soft, they were down about 15 percent versus the 50 percent for the stock funds.

Evil in the Boardroom

I decided to liquidate my stocks and sell cars when I needed to, to fund the company. The timing was not ideal to start a company with my net worth in a full nose dive and the economy in the tank.

We put a budget on the business of $250,000 with a maximum commitment of $500,000. I was pretty confident we could get a million dollars in business the first year; however, a number of things would soon transpire that would change all of our estimates—and none of them in a good way.

Pantera Global Technology was officially launched on Oct. 29, 2009, thirty days after the settlement with PEI. This was also the day PEI was sold to the Y factor company. I am not allowed to reveal the details of the settlement. We brought one of our account managers Chris on who had resigned from PEI, and he and I began making sales calls.

Virtually everyone I spoke with said they would take a look at it and try to help us get going. Chris and I booked a trip to New York to call on some customers and attend a local trade show. We were well received, but nobody was stepping up to the plate except for Lakeview, Staples, Ulta, Footlocker, Menemsha, and Shrader Martinez. I owe a debt of gratitude to these folks for their support. If I had known that many of my other so called friends from the past would not give us a chance no matter the price, I wouldn't have gone forward.

In late December 2009, we were served with notice of a lawsuit from the Y factor. The company was seeking an injunction against us. In the notice, it claimed to have my employment agreement, which it had purchased, as an asset and that I had committed numerous violations, including violation of the non-compete, stealing of customer information, tortuous interference of its business, stealing its trade secrets, and stealing the source code.

The Y factor named Bart and Chris as well with similar violations. The charges against me were annoying but didn't really bother me because my release and hold harmless was solid. The company may have had a case with the source code because I probably did have a copy of it somewhere. It was one of my routines to always have a copy off-site but I never had any intention of using it as it was outdated and not architected in a manner that would work for our business model.

The problem for Y factor was twofold. First, we didn't use its source code, and second, even if we did, I had a full release from PEI. There is a Tennessee statute that protects trade secrets, but something can only be considered a trade secret if it is treated as a trade secret. Jack had clearly lost the ability to claim a trade secret. He had shown the back end system without getting NDAs from any of the people he talked to. Numerous outsourced programmers had also seen it and worked on it. Being the scammer that he was, I was sure he would back date NDAs, but we had ample evidence and testimony that he hadn't met the standard for anyone to claim it as a trade secret. Secondly, I early on offered to let a third party review our code in exchange for dropping the suit when it was proved to be ours. The only real meat the Y factor had was against Chris's non-compete, and that was weak as long as he didn't call on the Y factor's customers. I was the lead sales person, and Chris was my account manager.

We did not go to the court appearance for the request for temporary injunction because the case had no merit for that sort of unreasonable request. Gil, the operations guy, who was now Jack's replacement, as Jack was not hired by the Y factor, would testify how I was killing their business, and so were Bart and Chris. He said how unfair it was to the company and all the employees to be subjected to that and how we were stealing everything they had worked for, etcetera.

We made a huge mistake not going to the hearing. The judge was clearly mentally challenged. Our attorney was caught off guard by her take on the situation and the broad reach she decided to take. She, in fact, did issue a temporary injunction against Bart and Chris. After that ruling, Chris decided to go to work for another company. Bart was handcuffed too. He was not allowed to service old PEI customers—and all the customers we had were prior PEI customers.

I was given a release fairly quickly once the Y factor realized what my deal actually was after reading our brief. We now had to prepare for trial. That meant they would do depositions on Bart and my old Lakeview partner! They decided to depose Kent. That may have been the best way for the situation to go down actually, because Bart's deposition revealed most of the facts I discussed here. They really didn't have anything other than the new knowledge that they had been duped by Jack. This lawsuit was going to be about which party was going to spend the most money.

My old assistant, who had lied about the lost credit card, was heard telling fellow employees that it was the Y factor's intent to sue me until I was broke and out of business. The Y factor's sales team was giving our customers a "heads up" that Pantera might be in trouble due to trying to defend the lawsuits.

I was very much looking forward to her and Gil's deposition. We also found out that Y factor didn't acquire Bart's and Chris's contracts until after the close of the sale. The fact that the Y factor said it owned the contracts but didn't acquire any of the company's liabilities, which would include the severance and vacation pay due, was a joke. I spent a lot of time crafting the deposition questions for my ex-assistant and Gil. They would be placed in a very bad situation when asked some of the questions we had prepared. They would be exposed to their new employer as being a part of Jack's misrepresentation scheme on the sale to Y factor in addition to making themselves open to a lawsuit against them personally.

I still had many contacts at PEI who were keeping me updated. Apparently when Y factor came in just after my departure and asked who the five salespeople were (they had all quit), Jack pointed his finger at a customer service rep, two account managers, the local account rep, and my ex-assistant. I am not sure how he explained the drastic sales dip, but shame on Y factor for not once reaching out to the founder of the company to understand the facts.

I often still wonder what the VC partners think about the superstar they hired as CEO. Did they know what he was up to, and do they now realize how incompetent and irresponsible he was? Knowing the philosophy of the VC mind-set, they probably only blame themselves for originally investing in me. They will never own up to the fact that they did not recognize and adjust for the recession as they should have. Plus they should have placed trust in the person they originally invested in.

Evil in the Boardroom

I am fairly confident that the Y factor quickly found out that the CEO had misrepresented the company. You see, there was a shift in the Y factor's strategy that started to occur as the depositions progressed.

To confirm my allegations of the way things may have gone down, I've included a screen shot at the end of the book (see image) of Jack's resumé as it's posted on the public side of LinkedIn. While not an outright lie, it is very telling about the way he represents himself and the things he has done. Who would question someone's skill when that person said he reduced overhead by $500,000 per month while retaining top company talent? WOW, amazing performance for a company that was doing 1.2 million dollars per month in sales.

The fact is, he did cut $500,000 from overhead, due to the fact that he lost one million dollars per month in sales with his new pricing strategy. The top talent he speaks of retaining can only be those same people he quickly named as salespeople during the due diligence period. (the customer service rep, two account managers, the local account rep, and my ex-assistant) As you can see, it is possible to totally destroy a company and still bolster your résumé if it's written in a manner of pure deception and self-promotion.

I stand by my position that, had the VCs checked their egos and their VC manual at the door at my last board meeting none of this would have happened. If my team would have been allowed the time needed to rectify things taking into account the economy and the damage done by the CEO we would have been a success, and I will prove it. Had the last capital raise, the "C" round, gone toward what it was supposed to, and the wildness of the CEO been corrected through his termination, the Pantera model would have been PEI's turnaround.

On the morning of the depositions for Gil and my previous assistant, with Bart present in Memphis, the Y factor's attorneys suggested starting settlement talks. Our attorney agreed. The depositions were canceled. I was not all that happy about it, but my attorney suggested it was prudent. That was late July 2010. The negotiations would drag on until November. They were clearly just trying to make Pantera/me spend money.

They had learned through Bart's deposition that we were doing nowhere near the volume they thought; hence, very little damage was done to their company. Even if they could get a ruling in their favor that meant little compensation. We had to start talks of filing a countersuit to end the situation.

As part of the settlement Bart, Chris, and any former employees of PEI who didn't go to work for Y factor were now free to work for Pantera in any capacity. Over one year later, we were finally free to get back to work without the distraction and restrictions.

We had spent much of that time focusing on the core product offering and expanding the functionality of the service. Our goal from day one was to come up with a system that was the future of construction technology, but also geared toward building community. By the beginning of 2011, we had a product that was clearly superior to the competition and had a zero price tag. That's correct: we decided to offer the software for free to our general contractors. We changed the name to PanteraTools and the focus on building a community of subcontractors and offering various software tools to them.

Unfortunately, the cost of the litigation, going over a year with very little revenue, the overhead of running the company and the outsourcing of technology, had taken their toll. I had now invested nearly $700,000 in a company that was generating very little revenue. Our only means of garnering revenue was through outsourced printing as a by-product of using the free software and from our Doc Clerk service, which charged a per file fee for document management.

My earlier visions of creating a million dollars in first-year revenue had been shattered by the lawsuit. We closed 2010 with only $300,000 in sales, and our monthly overhead was still consuming around $20,000 in extra cash per month. I had used nearly all of my life savings at that point. We needed to find a way to increase sales quickly to avoid going broke.

The remainder of the settlement from PEI was now due, and it was my intent to use that to cover the cash burn until sales got to a point of covering our costs. That $150,000 was needed to go into the company for us to survive. I was covering our living expense by renting out our large home as a vacation rental, and Debbie and I were renting a home from a wonderful man and fellow entrepreneur named Bus, who understood our predicament. Debbie had a couple of very nice real estate deals that came along, and we were scraping by and making the mortgage payments.

I had tried to get unemployment, but was denied despite two appeals. Apparently starting a new business disqualifies you from drawing on the money you contributed to the fund. Funny thing is, as the owner of the previous company, I actually paid double because of the employer contribution as well as the employee contribution. Thirty years of payments with no draw from the unemployment fund and I couldn't get a dime. They said I was not available for hire, because I was busy starting a new business. I explained that I could take care of my business and was available for full-time work, but that didn't cut it. Denied. So anyway, my attorney sent a letter to PEI asking for the remainder of the settlement, as our cash was almost gone and the payment was overdue.

19

PanteraTools.com, More Legal Problems

I had no reason to think that the payment on the balance due from PEI of the remaining settlement was going to be easy to collect, but I certainly never thought I would have to start a new lawsuit to collect it. My thought was that at most a couple of letters from the attorney, a few phone calls, and that would be it. After all, it was a large venture capital firm, and I had an ironclad agreement.

The letters we wrote were not being responded to and it became necessary to bring in another attorney from Memphis to put pressure on the firm to pay up. The feedback from the attorneys on the other side was extremely strange and perplexing. They asked for copies of the signature pages from the original agreement, then the whole document, and then they did not respond for weeks, which forced more letters. That all started to cost a lot of money that I, frankly, was not able to pay, and I explained the problem to the attorneys. We all felt it was just a matter of time until PEI paid, so they continued working.

Meanwhile, I woke up one morning to find a notice in my e-mail from my bank that my checking account balance was $138,000 overdrawn. How could that be? I had about $6,000 in it. After calling the bank, I was told that the $6,000 had been seized from my account by the state of New York for a tax lien and that the overdraft represented the balance due.

It took most of the day on the phone with numerous people from the state of New York to finally get some answers. The state had done an audit of PEI in August 2009 after my departure and determined that taxes were due on all product shipped to customers in New York because we had an office there. I knew that and said that we always paid the tax, and besides, why were they coming after me for it? With some desperate pleading to a very understanding woman at the state tax department, I was given the name of the actual auditor. That was something she was not supposed to reveal, and I knew that even with that information, the auditor would probably not talk to me, but I had no choice other than to try.

What happened next pretty much had me throwing in the towel. I was out of money, the company was losing money, neither my son Bart nor I had been paid, and on top of that, now I had a huge tax lien with a garnishee on my bank account, mounting legal bills, and very little hope. The auditor, who was initially very matter of fact and unsympathetic to my situation, allowed me to explain what had occurred. At the same time he explained to me the series of events that occurred after my departure.

The audit was a routine audit done by the state, and the timing happened to coincide with Jack's negotiations with the Y factor's purchase of the company. The audit revealed that tax was charged and paid on the product but not on the shipping.

Evil in the Boardroom

The state of New York and others charge sales tax on any shipping charges that are not a direct pass-through. Our shipping charges could not be known at the time of purchase due to variable factors such as residential surcharges and fuel surcharges and the fact that we marked up our shipping rates. That was the tax that was now due.

I explained to the auditor that the COO at the time of the infraction had hired a consultant. That person said tax was not due. My controller showed me the actual tax filing. When I saw that the line item for tax on shipping had a zero in it, I stated that it looked like we owed tax and I refused to sign it as CEO. That resulted in a screaming match with the COO, who insisted that I sign it. I again refused. I read the fine print, and it was clear to me, despite his consultant's representation that no tax was due, there was tax owing. He then ordered our controller to sign the tax form, which she did.

I informed the auditor that those events were all done after the company was reincorporated after the series "B" funding therefore that I had no personal responsibility. I had gone as far as removing the personal guarantee language on the state form when we originally applied for the state license.

He said none of it mattered. They had sent numerous demands to PEI as well as to my home address, and any of my rebuttals could have been addressed at that time. The money was now due, a judgment and a tax lien were in place, and they would continue to come after me, including going after my house if necessary. He also believed that challenging in court was probably not going to work. The best I could do was to work out a payment plan with the man in charge of the collection. He did tell me, however, that I should document my claims on the official tax lien website for reference.

I did as he asked, though I called him back a couple of days later, having thought through the details, and asked how the lien could possibly be fair in light of the situation. I had had no idea that the audit had been done, I did not receive the notice (it had been sent to a home address I had moved away from six years prior), I had refused to sign the tax form, and lastly and most importantly, had I been there, I would have had the company pay the tax. Add to that the fact that Jack surely knew about the situation and must have simply tossed the notices in the garbage, ignoring the state. This was just another example of Jack deliberately trying to hurt me yet again. One of my remaining contacts at PEI had informed me that Jack had actually thrown all of the notices into a corner in an empty office.

The auditor had taken the time to read my posting on the web filing form and listened intently to what I had to say. I sensed that he did sympathize, but there wasn't much he could do. I let him know that I was going to reach out to the senior VC and try to work with him to send out invoices to the customers who were not charged the tax, collect the tax due, and send it to the state. He asked that I again post that to the site as well and to keep him informed of my progress.

I sent an e-mail to the senior VC explaining the entire situation. I included new facts I received from the controller at the time, and the accountant that the COO used for his determination of no tax due. I even sent an e-mail to the former COO asking for help. The response from the VC was a one-liner that his CFO was handling it and there was nothing he could do. The ex-COO, never replied. A second e-mail to the VC explaining that rebilling the invoices and writing off non-payments could probably resolve most of the lien fell on unsympathetic deaf ears. It was my problem. I added that information to my web filing as well.

About a week later, the auditor called me to say that things were progressing and the payment plan needed to be worked out. With desperation settling in, I let him know that I would agree to whatever they determined. He could see by my web postings and my efforts to correct other people's mistakes, that I had been hung out to dry. My demise would help remove me as a competitor to the new company that was surely paying PEI (the VC) based on an earn-out deal, so I was essentially beaten.

They had taken my company; I would also lose my life savings and would go bankrupt with no chance of employment due to my age and the recession. The last question I asked him was why only me? Why weren't they trying to get some money from the other officers and so-called responsible parties? His simple answer was that they had been given my bank account information somewhere along the line and didn't have the other parties' information.

Two things happened here. One, I had again been set up again by my ex-assistant, who had obviously given them my bank account information but no one else's and two, I was about to go on a mission to get the man some more information. Within two days he had all he needed to file lien notices on at least three other individuals, and he let me know that he would proceed to do so and would see where that took us.

Within two weeks I received a conference call from the auditor and the state saying that a settlement was now being offered by the other parties. The state was willing to close the case if I accepted responsibility for one-quarter of the settlement amount. I didn't understand why I should agree to that when it was the company that owed the money, and it was surely the company that would now pay the other three liens on the personal accounts. They were also doing nothing to try to help collect the tax. They let me know that it was the end of the line; there was nothing more they could do, and the amount was greatly reduced. I signed the settlement with the state.

We were now well into March 2011, and I had spent most of my time trying to collect the PEI settlement payment due, dealing with the tax lien, and training a new salesperson with zero experience. I was also running the company, helping with new product, moving from house to house, and working on a business plan.

The "business plan" was to do the one thing I really didn't want to do, which was to bring in an investor. If the final settlement payment from PEI came through shortly, we should be able to make it last until the company became profitable; if it didn't, we needed investor money fairly soon.

20

PanteraTools – Lift Off

What I hadn't mentioned earlier is that, during Christmas 2010, just after the start-up of Pantera, Debbie and I made our annual pilgrimage to Christmas Day Mass at the local Catholic church. I never looked forward to it, but I usually felt good on the drive home. I had fallen away from religion in light of my so-called secular education and common sense beliefs. The Roman Catholic Church sure wasn't helping, with a scandal seemingly every month. On the way home from Mass that Christmas I told Debbie that I would like to go more often. It did make me feel really good afterward. She suggested we again visit a nearby Bible church we had been to once or twice a few years back. I said that would be great, let's start next week. And we did. We actually have gone every single week from that day forward.

On the business side of things, there were now a few more players on the scene with similar products. The recession, coming up on three years old, the continuing rumor mill, the lack of help from old, friendly customers, numerous failures on deadlines of software, the lack of sales, plus no permanent place to set up an office were really taking a toll.

We had to build sales fast, and the only way to do it was to get in front of the customer and come up with a new approach. The free software model was not working. I had spent five months training an attractive (mandatory in the industry) young girl in all aspects of the job. I had done that successfully numerous times before and decided to go back to basics.

I taught her every detail on the product, the customer, and the industry. The sales techniques, the methods, and the follow-up that was required as well. She was ready to go out and meet face-to-face with potential customers. I also decided that we would do the road show together. It was much easier to get an appointment if you were bringing the CEO or president to meet the perspective customer. That also gave me the chance to further her training by having her watch me do the introduction and explain my history and knowledge of the industry.

That had always worked for me in the past, and I was willing to spend the money and time to get out there and do it again. The other thing we decided to do at the same time was to emphasize the Doc Clerk paid services, not as an option as we had in the past, but as a mandatory piece of the offering. We would end up being about the same price as the competition except that the customer got document management as part of the deal. The others didn't provide that or charged even more for that feature.

It was May 2011, and in two-and-a-half days, we called on six clients in Southern California. The meetings went well, I ended up doing 90 percent of the presentations, and we got soft verbal commitments or curious inclinations from all. All that was left for the salesperson to do was the follow-up and to bring them on board.

Evil in the Boardroom

That was something I was weak at. It was a good plan, it went well, and three weeks after the trip, not a single person was on board. She just did not have the skills.

I let the sales girl go in June and made calls on my own via the phone and started running out of options. I had finished the business plan and sent it out to a number of firms. I made three or four presentations including one I considered a game changer with a huge content provider that took a very sharp and quick interest. It was a perfect strategic play that would give us at least one million in cash as well as a huge community of general contractors and, most importantly, the name-branding power of partnering with a large company that would instantly legitimize Pantera.

Bart and I were called down to Atlanta to meet with the CEO and his VP of business development for an all-day, not-to-be-disturbed meeting to figure out the deal points and the action plan for a partnership. The meeting went incredibly well, and we were told that we would have an action plan and preliminary agreement within ten days. True to their word, it arrived on schedule and encompassed everything we had talked about and included a few other facets we had not thought of. They also mentioned that the investment would come in the form of cash, earned equity from providing services, and infrastructure, or a combination of the three. We would discuss the valuation during the next step.

We agreed 100 percent to the action plan, and I said I was open to talking about numerous methods or means of calculating the valuation for the investment. They thanked us for the feedback and told us that we would not hear back from them for three weeks because they were busy with two trade shows.

I waited four weeks and when I didn't hear anything back, I reached out to them. I was told that they were very close to putting something together and needed another week. Bart and I were very excited. It looked as if things might finally be falling into place.

Our sales climbed as our current customers got busier, and I was able to close a number of accounts with the new Doc Clerk plan. I had not closed a single large account yet, but we were growing at about 10 percent per month.

After not hearing from our potential partner for close to another two weeks, I called and was told that the CEO was in Europe working on the deal. I found that a little strange. He had said that he didn't need approval from his international HQ for anything under one million dollars. I convinced myself that it could only be good news.

Four days later I received an abrupt and curt phone call from the CEO telling me that the deal was not going to happen. He would not give me an explanation, only that a decision had been made and our deal was not going through. A week later he called me back and was more cordial. He let me know they had done a deal with another company similar to ours (at least in their eyes), that he admired what I had done, and that we should stay in contact, as the deal did not preclude them from doing something with us down the road. Oh well.

We were now into July, and sales were about double the year before but nowhere near what we needed. I made the decision to try one more time to bring on a salesperson. This time I decided to try someone who had worked for me before as an account manager and knew the industry well. We were still counting on the fact that the settlement, now long overdue, would be paid anytime. Our account manager, Sue, was now closing new business as well, but ever so slowly.

I got slammed again when yet another demand letter from my attorney to PEI for payment resulted in a letter back from PEI threatening to sue me for basically all of the things I had been released from prior. That was very bizarre and made no sense whatsoever. I asked my attorney to call the other side and let them know we had the resources to take them to court and that we would. Yes, it was a slight bluff, but at that point, I was confident my attorney would work through it with me. I asked him to also try to find out what the strategy was during the conversation.

Ted, my Memphis attorney, made the call and said that the response was that the two sides, PEI and Y factor, were not getting along well. Apparently numerous things had come up over the last year that were preventing earn-out payments from Y factor to PEI, and that it looked as if there might never be any payments.

Knowing that was completely possible now that the people at Y factor were beginning to understand whom they had dealt with, I was convinced I would never see a dime. Jack had probably made even more misrepresentations than I could have imagined. The opposing attorney closed the conversation with a statement suggesting, "Your client should be lucky he got what he got, and we have let bygones be bygones till this point, but if he pushes this we can get real nasty."

The number of laps I have paced in the various houses while talking to my attorneys on the phone cannot be calculated, but I guarantee it's a marathon. I can't sit on a phone and endure that type of talk without pacing.

We had very little left in the tank, but I asked my attorney to try to get the accounting that was also due us as part of the settlement. We would then determine what action to take and whether to pursue or not. Y factor's attorney complied—and made a huge mistake.

They sent us a spreadsheet that showed—based on the earn-out deal we were tied to with our release—that the payments were, in fact, owed to PEI, in accordance with the earn-out provision, and overdue. My payment was tied to the earn-out as I was the first beneficiary to any payments. When we asked PEI's attorney why they hadn't been paid he said we would have to go after Y factor for that information but that there were extenuating circumstances that wouldn't allow it based on some unknown liabilities and such. We contacted Y factor to let its management and attorneys know that I was a beneficiary to the payments they had not made and that were owed and that we were suing PEI for nonpayment and they would be a party to the suit. During that conversation the Y factor attorney said that I was not a beneficiary to the deal his client had signed with PEI.

My attorney said, "That's absurd, I'm looking at your CEO's signature saying that the Adamson release and agreement were a component of the closing documents dated September of 2009."

Evil in the Boardroom

"Well," stated the other attorney, "I'm looking at a sale agreement dated June 2010 that does not list Adamson at all." We asked for the document and it was sent right over.

Apparently the original deal was so misrepresented that Y factor had demanded a new sale agreement to take into account uncollectable receivables (most likely Jack's new pricing policy that no one would pay), lost accounts, and numerous other unknowns. Without it they were going to sue. PEI complied to some form of a new deal based on earnings instead of the previous one that was based on sales, but they failed to include me as a beneficiary to the deal or even as a third-party liability to the corporation. They just drafted a whole new deal and cut me out completely.

We called PEI's attorney and let him know that things had just taken a dramatic turn. They had breached the agreement and signed the new sale agreement "personally" without my permission. We would be suing PEI, Y factor, and the "signers of the documents personally" for the money owed plus damages and any other charges that they might be subject to.

That was September 2011. We were in discussions with both attorneys now, and it was obvious to me that they had made a very large mistake. They asked if we could settle. We agreed, and it took two months to complete a deal. As I stated before I cannot reveal the terms or the existence of any agreement nor will I disparage the parties which I have not done, other than to retell the events in an actual and truthful manner as they occurred. I have also not used real names for any of the parties or used actual company names of those involved to further protect myself.

I will go on to state that the VC's I dealt with were not doing anything spiteful or particularly wrong. The advice here is to have terms that are agreeable and to deal with people who you believe will treat you fairly. I had been advised by my attorney to fight back hard on the 5 year redemption privilege clause. Who could have ever predicted the worst recession in history that made that clause so impactful.

My VC's would not sway one iota from the VC 101 text book and that was tough. There are plenty of good Venture Capital firms out there, just be cautious and do your homework by talking to some of the other founders in firms they have invested in. My big complaint with my investors was their failure to acknowledge and deal with a really bad CEO choice, choosing instead to ignore the mistake and press on no matter the outcome to avoid admitting they were wrong.

If I had had the resources, we could have had a very strong case to recover the millions in equity that had been lost. It was very clear they intended to not pay the remaining settlement money owed, and for that reason alone, they should have been sued. However, I wanted to move on, and even if the attorneys would do the work on a contingency basis, I did not want to have any further dealings with the VCs.

While the negotiations were underway, I was in the process of doing another road show of sales presentations identical to the one in May, except this time to the New York area with my former employee in tow. We called on seven companies on a three-day trip. The presentations were identical to the ones four months earlier, but the reaction was not the same. The response from the last trip

Evil in the Boardroom

had been somewhat positive and good overall, but the response this time was overwhelming.

We closed five of the seven while in their offices. Full on commitments, projects, address books, and orders. What was the difference?

Sales doubled overnight, to the point where by December 2011, our servers were overloaded. My team was working furiously to build new equipment, modify software, and stabilize the website.

I had to ask the two salespeople to stop selling and concentrate on customer service until we got things under control. We were a few weeks away from turning on paid downloads to our subcontractor community, which would show whether or not the company would skyrocket. That would have to wait until early 2012.

What was different in September versus May? Try as I might to find an answer, there was only one thing that was different. I had said a prayer before each day began and asked God for help that day. The results were amazing.

21

Life Lessons and loose ends.

While writing this book it became clear to me that it was really only about twenty years ago, at the age of thirty-seven, that I became elementarily able to think about running a business. For the ten years prior to that I was simply learning, whether it was from my mother for sales, Vic for negotiations, Gene for pragmatism or Don Jr. for organization. In my early life experiences, I went from being a really good kid at a Catholic school to fighting and stealing and their consequences and it all formed a strong amount of common sense. I believe if a person has good common sense, the ability to learn, and one or two great career mentors, he or she can be successful. Keeping what you earned and being happy with your life is something entirely different, however.

When we were rolling at State Construction, life was grand and a ball of fun. For the first time in my life, I didn't worry about being able to pay my monthly bills. It's not as if I was crazy rich, but I could live a lifestyle that was very good by the standards I had grown up with and compared to the people I was surrounded by at the time. I really had all I needed and all I had ever hoped for.

Always working extremely hard, I still had lots of time for fun, travel, and entertainment. The only missing component was not controlling my own destiny. Although I enjoyed working as an employee, I would become frustrated by management decisions that, at times, I didn't agree with and at other times threatened the security of my future.

I started to get a strong urge to go out on my own but felt very loyal to my employer, so I looked for other means to scratch the itch. That is how Alert Service and Expicon came to be. The itch then got stronger when I sought to go into the retail business. Ultimately, the urge to go on my own was fulfilled not by me but by my employer's bad decisions.

The extremes of my wild young life were starting to mellow a bit. No more outrunning the police in a car chase or walking steel beams two hundred feet in the air. Gone was standing on a motorcycle seat and driving with no hands through downtown.

We no longer went out at lunchtime for drinks instead of a meal. Sometimes it's hard to understand how popular that was for a very long time. While working in the factory or on construction jobsites, it was an everyday event to eat your sandwich on the way back to work after slamming three beers and a couple of shots. That went on for many years in the trades, and it was the same once I moved to an office environment. The only difference was that the drink of choice was now a fancy cocktail. There was no such thing as alcohol and drug tests back then, and if you got pulled over, you were always given a warning and sent on your way as long as you were courteous.

The nine-year run with Plan Express was an extremely stressful point in my life, personally as well as professionally but I thrived on it. Not only did I commute every other week to Memphis, I worked out of our Tempe office when in Arizona and I also did a large number of trade shows.

My stepbrother Wayne has been in and out of my life during all of my business start-ups. I have always tried to employ him in some way. Unfortunately, it has been a continual battle with drugs and rehab. He is one of the hardest workers I have ever met and has a huge heart but continues to relapse. I have answered the call to run out to the nearest Western Union for a quick desperation money transfer far too many times.

My father and I talk nowadays, and he has made attempts to be more a part of my life. I hold no grudge and am happy to involve him in my life, but there is an awkwardness that is hard to overcome, especially when many of our conversations ultimately end with "there is a lot you don't know" or "my next wife would not allow me to make contact." Really? That is disappointing to hear, to say the least. It would be far better to just man up.

My son Clint is married and seems very happy, although it looks as if there are no grandchildren in my future, and for this, I am a bit sad. My sister, Gena, is happily married and content; although we don't see each other much, we remain close. Bart and I are still working together, and he is a very large part of Pantera.

My friend Dean was torn in the dispute during the last days of PEI and believed my ex-assistant's rendition that backed Jack, which hurt me deeply. He was another mentor whom I admired and respected as much as anyone I have ever known.

Evil in the Boardroom

I also feel bad for the original series "A" investors. Their terms and patience would have allowed a nice return on their investment had we not gotten involved with the vicious series "B" group. My independent board member and I remain close, and I have asked him to be a part of Pantera. Numerous other bridges were burned and some repaired. Needless to say, it was quite a learning experience. Jim M has done well, and we are still in touch.

I could go on but why? Let's get back to business.

22

So You're Ready to Start a Business?

When starting a business, it is very important to have a support structure around you. Having key employees, close friends, and family there for you as an emotional cheering squad can get you though many of the difficult times that will be placed in front of you. However...

Many people think that starting a business is easy and a sure way to success. They read about Bill Gates or Steve Jobs and get the totally wrong idea. They perhaps hear about a contractor who just built a huge mansion and is raking it in. These are the one-tenth of the 1 percent of businesses that take off like a rocket and have all the right ingredients for success. That is not going to happen to you.

Believe me: it is extremely difficult to start a business from scratch. A key statistic to keep in mind is that, after five years, only one out of five will still be in business. Of those 20 percent, only 10 percent will be successful, with the definition of success meaning to provide more than a regular income. That means only two out of one hundred will do well and eighty will go broke. The remaining eighteen companies will have owners who bust their butts, work incredibly long hours, and endure great hardships in order to make ends meet. The key to changing these numbers is to learn from the mistakes and the successes of a mentor or someone like the serial entrepreneur I've become. I have made plenty of mistakes and had a few successes.

Why do so many good ideas fail? The answer is not as simple as the question, but I will give some insight on how to vastly improve your chances. Number one is to ask yourself, "Why is this such a great idea?" I have said it is important to have a cheering squad, but this can also hurt you if this same support structure gives you plain blind faith. Unless your company is a brand-new invention the world has been waiting for, there are many ways for you to parse out the viability of your idea prior to the business plan stage. But never move forward without a business plan—an investment-grade business plan.

You must understand that many good ideas fail due to lack of funds, a bad economy, or because you don't anticipate the competition from others copying your great idea and carving into your market. If you rely on a partner or a key employee, you may fall victim to his or her greed or need for control. Money changes people in ways that cannot be overstated. There are other things that are totally out of your control and cannot be anticipated, such as the introduction of a new technology or product making yours obsolete. You can be sidelined by a simple misfortune of a bad event or bad publicity.

Over the course of the twenty years from the late 1980s to 2009, I started eight companies and drew up business plans for six more. At least a dozen more didn't make the business plan stage for one reason or another. That is more than two dozen well-thought-out business ideas that I took to various stages of completion. Some at great expense. In order to do that and actually run the eight companies that did get to the stage of an actual business required much trial and error.

If you are going to start a business, don't do so unless you can give your utmost dedication and your heart and soul to making it work. Save the slacking off for after your business is up, successful, and running on its own.

The companies I started were all in the million-dollar sales range and up. The biggest company was my construction company, which ultimately grew to over one hundred million dollars in sales. The size of those businesses is not all that material, though, depending on the industry. It isn't very hard to be a general contractor doing millions in sales as opposed to selling one million dollars' worth of pizzas or gift items. The key is to understand what it takes to start the company, to actually run the business, and ultimately to grow it and exit it.

Most young entrepreneurs do not fully understand the cost structure of running a legitimate business. I didn't. Dealing with insurance premiums, workman's compensation, state and federal withholding, unemployment and Medicare payments, health care costs, vacations, paid holidays, liability, triple net rents, accounting fees, maintenance, marketing, bandwidth, uncollectable receivables, cash flow management, taxes, and interest were all foreign to me. Others always handled those things; I just went out and solicited the work and ran the jobs to make money. This is why a proper business plan is so important.

Evil in the Boardroom

Let's go back to whether or not your idea is good. As an example, a great many people want to own a restaurant or be in the food service industry. They go to a particular restaurant and see it full of people on a weekend evening, and thinking they can provide as good or better service and food, they decide that they can share in the apparent wealth. They are sure that the owner is raking in the cash. There is another one opening across town, there is talk of franchising, and the owner just bought a new house and a new car. All you need to do is put your genius into the menu, think up a cool name and logo, charge better prices, and of course, provide better service than the other restaurant, and you will do great.

This must happen every single hour of every day because restaurants come and go more than any other business. Why does that happen? The answer is that there was no plan. Or at least not a plan that was legitimate. A proper business plan would involve more than counting the tables in the restaurant and determining sales by conservatively dividing by two. While this may sound conservative, it isn't even close. Most businesses only budget for six months' planning until they achieve breakeven. That is just plain crazy and a recipe for losing your life savings.

The opposite happens fairly often and can be equally deceiving. You witness a brand-new enterprise open to standing-room-only crowds and are convinced that you can do the same. Many times a new restaurant will open and become attractive because of the fact that it is new. Unless customers are blown away by the food, the service, and the prices, the newness will wear off, and without quick correction of overhead and a step up in service and food, you will be doomed. The biggest mistake people make is underestimating the cash required to sustain the business until profitability.

By spending the time to do a proper investment-grade business plan, you will discover nearly all of the questions that must be answered and solved to minimize the risk of starting the business. Your idea will be explained in the executive summary. It will be further examined in your marketing strategy. It will be protected in how you create barriers to entry for competitors. These will be backed up by doing market research for the sector and measuring results against your projections. You will do a top down and bottom up sales forecast to show that the overhead is in proportion to sales and that your minimum required overhead does not force you to add sales to cover it on paper.

Build the projections and the cost modeling like you were going to raise money to fund the project, even if you don't intend to have partners. Solicit opinions from others in the sector. Don't worry about sharing your great idea with a few friends or relatives for fear someone may steal your idea. If your idea is that easy to copy, you should think twice about doing it in the first place. A business success or failure is based 90 percent on the people behind it, not just some cool idea.

The businesses that I started were all in areas that I had knowledge in. To start a business without previous experience in that industry is suicidal unless you are investing in a franchise or buying an existing successful business and the owner will assist in training. Sometimes a detailed plan is not required if you happen to be fortunate enough to have purchase orders and commitments before you start. You already know approximately what your volumes will be and this will save you time in the research needed to project sales.. This should not, however, prevent you from putting together all of the other aspects of the business plan.

Evil in the Boardroom

It also needs to be pointed out that, just because you do a thorough business plan, it doesn't mean you'll be successful even if all the numbers add up, and everyone agrees that the market is ripe for the taking. Sometimes instances will surface that cannot be accounted for.

Employee issues are probably the most dangerous for a small business. No shows or poor customer service can really hurt. A disgruntled employee can spell disaster. If the problem employee is a friend or relative, you have an even bigger problem. The other unknown is the reaction of your customers at seeing your success and wanting to compete. Remember the restaurant story.

Earlier I wrote about the start-up of Call of the Wild, the high-end motorcycle boutique. It opened just prior to the explosion of the Harley Davidson market. Unfortunately, two other shops opened within our first year, both within five miles of our location. The business plan was proper, the cash reserves were double the plan amount, and we opened on time and according to plan. We reached breakeven within six months, at which point the other shops started opening and sharing from the same pie.

That could have easily been a large failure had I not ended up selling the business to a wealthy competitor who was doing it just for fun. What I didn't count on was that guy deciding to bankrupt the company prior to paying me off. Just because someone appears to have, or actually has, a lot of money doesn't mean he or she won't stiff you, leaving you with the excuse of "it's just business" to justify the action. That particular guy owned many cancer treatment centers across the United States but decided to not live up to his commitment just because he could. The lesson here is to always get a personal guarantee at a minimum.

The most important thing of all, though, is the amount of cash you have available to start your business. Whatever you think you need, you are probably wrong. I have never started a business not using more cash than I initially figured, and I have never met anyone else who has. So many variables affect cash that you can't cover them all in the business plan without having it look like a disclaimer from an SEC filing.

Here are examples of things that could use your cash that you didn't count on: Excess cost comes in the form of construction costs overages, delays, fines, and lawsuits. Sales don't come as fast as you projected, or proper marketing was not done due to the failure of others. You can do everything according to plan, but you cannot plan for other people's failures. How about a web developer who did well for a colleague but suddenly doesn't deliver or gets too busy? The marketing firm you hired ended up producing a brochure that looks like garbage. Your very best colleague, who promised you his business, decides he must wait to give you the business until you're successful in order to not jeopardize his own business.

This is the stuff that tempers your spirit or destroys it. I would have never guessed that starting Pantera would result in nearly $200,000 in unanticipated legal fees. Could your small business take a hit like that? It's unfortunate, but these things happen, and you must have your eyes wide open before you start.

Evil in the Boardroom

I hate to sound so pessimistic, but these are the facts and the reasons so many businesses fail. If you have all this covered, your plan is solid, and you have the cash, running your own show is one of the most rewarding things you can do. Or if you're like me, it's about the only way you can make money because you find yourself simply unable to work for someone else.

23

Do You Need Investors?

If your business plan calls for raising money in order to fund it, you are entering a whole different area that I detailed earlier in the book regarding angel investors or venture capital, starting in the Plan Express saga of the Good, the Bad, the Ugly, and Put a fork in it, it's done.

Going down that road means you will not own all of the company, and you must be comfortable with that. Further cash draws to make up for sales shortfalls or to capture market share will dilute your ownership percentage even more. If you have the mind-set that it is your company and you could never own a minority piece of it, do not take other people's money.

If the only way to launch your plan and make it a success is to go that route then you must seek advice from someone very knowledgeable. They'll be able to help you with the deal points of a term sheet or the close of any stock sale. Most business attorneys have no clue about the implications of liquidation preference multiples or redemption privilege timelines and the end effect. Attorneys who specialize in financings are few and far between and are very expensive.

Evil in the Boardroom

Entrepreneurs tend to get all tied up in the pre money or post money valuation of the company and give up valuable terms that will far outweigh the importance of the initial valuation. I am carefully considering starting a consulting firm that will cater to entrepreneurs seeking help with building their plans, doing the solicitation, and negotiating the deal. I found almost no help in the libraries or on the Internet on the subject other than pages and pages of scammers on the internet.

There is a whole industry developing around firms that will do what I am considering, but they require cash up front. They say the cash is used to do the due diligence required to help put together the plan and solicit it to the proper investors. In addition to the cash up front, they will ask for stock in the company, usually in the form of warrants. A deeper look will show that they make their money based on the up-front fee rather than success fees. I could understand an hourly fee not to exceed a few thousand dollars and getting stock options or warrants after a successful financing, but many of these firms are looking for $50,000 up front, and I just don't believe that is necessary.

If, by the time this book is published, I have decided to do this type of work, such as business plan creation, financial consultation, or just providing an opinion on a new venture idea, my contact information will be at the end of the book. If I do it, I will tell you right up front if I believe in your idea. If I didn't believe it would work I would not take the job. The people you find in the VC forums will take your money no matter what they believe.

24

Your Most Important Partner

As I pointed out earlier in the book, I was raised a Catholic, as were my children, but found myself gradually falling away from church, prayer, and religion in general. My hard work and dedication to each business paid off financially, but not without a lot of turmoil. As easy as it may seem, it was not. All-night preparations for board meetings, frequent arduous travel, very high-pressure tactics from investors, and a stressful home life can make it all seem worthless at times.

I think the stress and hopelessness of seeing your business implode due to the missteps of others, the multiple lawsuits, the tax problems from the state of New York, and the additional stress of trying to start a brand-new business in a serious recession took me to the point of near collapse both mentally and physically. They say God wants to build on a solid foundation, and many times the only way to do that is to tear everything down in preparation for the rebuild.

For me the day came unexpectedly. I was sitting on an airplane searching my Kindle trying to find another book to read before the plane boarded. I had just finished the autobiography of Benjamin Franklin, which was a free book on Kindle. Looking at other books that might be available for free, I found the King James Version of the Bible. Time was running out, and I would be asked to turn my device off quickly, so I went ahead and downloaded the Bible. I started reading Genesis shortly after takeoff.

In all the years of my upbringing, I had never read the entire Bible. I had memorized the Mass in Latin way back when and knew all the Catholic prayers, but my Bible study was just a few verses at a time during Mass on Sundays or later at Christmas and Easter. After reading on the plane that day, I decided that I would read the entire sixty-six books of the Bible from start to finish. Why? I do not know, but I was compelled to finish it.

It took me nearly five months. I'm sure I could have done it faster, but there were times when the frustration of some of the events in the Bible, mostly in the Old Testament, would slow me down or make me go back and research what I was reading. I was fortunate enough to have some people in my life to help me out. Nancy, a high school friend whom I reconnected with on a reunion website, and Julie, whom I had met through our fitness center were available to answer some of the questions I had during some of the tough reading spots. They made things much easier to understand. I admire both of these women and their connection with God, and they helped me immensely.

I do not recommend reading the Bible this way. There are probably much better ways of understanding the Bible than doing it in sequential order. Get a bible with study guides and timelines. There is also suggested ways of reading them in a better order at the end of most of them. I remember reading a verse one night that defined wisdom as the fear of God and the shunning of evil. This and numerous other impactful verses pointed out by these two great women made it possible for me to begin to savor the word.

When I said earlier how I had drifted away from the church, I did not say how far I had drifted. When you get caught up in secular politics and the so-called intellectual crowd, discussions about evolution and Jesus can be very provocative and are therefore avoided. Never mix business with pleasure, and don't discuss politics or religion is a familiar saying. I pretty much followed that strategy until I read the Dan Brown book *The Da Vinci Code.*. It's a wonderfully written story about lies and deceit spun by the church and incredibly enough, I thought this fictitious book gave me justification for my split from religion. I shared that with my kids, and they too believed that much about Christianity was contrived. For me, at the time, those were just good talking points and again just an excuse for me to not go to church. On a cool summer night a couple of years prior, at the height of my career, I was enjoying dinner with a friend named David and his wife, Kathleen, when the subject of religion came up. David was a very wealthy car dealer who had lost everything but came back to become extremely successful. David talked about how he and Kathleen read the Bible together. I said I thought that was nice but that I had doubts as to the authenticity of the Old and New Testaments. David told me that, unless I believed that Jesus was the only way to get to heaven, I was going to hell. I told him how ridiculous that was, at which point he let me know we would not be seeing each other again.

I was flabbergasted but thought, hey, this further proves that the Bible is nutty. How could a good God send good people to hell? What if a Buddhist who only did good all his life but didn't believe in Jesus died? He would go to hell? I don't think so. Anyway, you could see where my head was at the time. (David still doesn't have everything right in my opinion today either, by the way.)

As I said earlier, I started to go to church every Sunday during that time of reading the Bible. It was wonderful, and finally the day came when I accepted Jesus. What does this mean? For me it was the repentance of my sins and the acceptance that Jesus died for my sins and rose to heaven. The Holy Spirit hit me right in the chest. I knew it and I felt it. I cried. I was reborn. That was just before Easter 2011. Knowledge of the Bible is very important and makes the journey easier, but a good church with a powerful pastor makes it a cinch. The church we are currently attending is unlike any I had ever been to.

As I stated earlier during the time that Pantera was struggling and there were all the lawsuits, I was reading the bible. We started training and setting up meetings for the September trip to New York. Seven meetings, five closes. Same presentation, same product. The only difference was that I had prayed to God before each day began, asking for his help. And it worked. I actually left each meeting in awe at the response. Kim, my new sales person and I were dazed at how well we were received and how quickly clients wanted to come on board.

Sales over the next month started increasing substantially. I asked for God's help in settling the lawsuit, and by mid-November, the agreement was being drafted.

I decided to step up my church activities by attending prayer groups and other functions. Debbie and I joined a small group that met weekly to do Bible study.

With sales starting to approach the point where I could stop writing checks to fund the business, I asked for guidance and help. What could I do for God and the church? That's when I was inspired to write this book. My promise is to dedicate this book to God and any profits from the book to the church. I began to make notes for the book in September 2011.

In November I contacted Gene Sunday, my former boss and then partner, to let him know that I was a follower of Jesus and would be visiting my hometown the next week. He asked if I would like to join him and Don Jr. at a Bible study. Don Jr.? Yes, he too had become a Christian. I went to the Bible study with them and, afterward, we went to a Cracker Barrel restaurant for breakfast, where we prayed together before eating. That picture will be forever carved into my brain, and it would certainly stun a lot of people.

Becoming a Christian is not without its surprises. When some of my friends heard of my conversion, they were suddenly hard to find. Many more took issue with it, as they felt they were too intelligent to believe in God.

The funny thing is, the older I get and the more knowledge I accumulate, I realize how little I know and no offense, how little the critics know. I read that there are over 700,000 books in the Smithsonian. If a person lived long enough and had perfect recall or a photographic memory and read a book a week for his or her entire life, he or she would still *not* know over 99 percent of what is in that library.

This statement has nothing to do with what you believe in. It is meant to point out that none of us is smart enough to claim intelligence alone as a factor for non believe.

Evil in the Boardroom

Some people don't believe in God and ask for proof. I say give me proof there is no God. The response usually has to do with seemingly tragic events, death, wars and so on. A good God would not do that. However, there is the concept of free will and the fact that if no bad things ever happened, we would already be in heaven.

By December 2011 the lawsuit had been settled and sales had grown to a point where I was able to put myself on the payroll. At a Sunday service we were asked to give God a test. The message was that, if we shared with God, we would be rewarded. I know this to be true. I remembered seeing Gene write a check to the church for a lot of money one year. I had asked him why he gave so much. He stated that the more he gave, the more he got back. I decided to tithe, in advance, based on my future new pay status and took the check to the church office. I cannot remember a time of feeling so fulfilled with giving.

I now wonder how my life would have been impacted had I asked for God's help in my other business ventures. No matter, it is all part of the plan, and it is my hope that this book inspires you to reach whatever goals you set and that some of the guidelines given here help you to achieve those goals without the hardship or need of learning through tough trials that I had to face so many times.

25

Pantera Moves into 2012

Project Leads

I am actually very proud of where the company is now. Although it has been over two years since the company started, it is only in the last year that we have been free to run the company unhindered by lawsuits (except for cash).

The success of the company has actually had some impact we were not prepared for. By mid-December 2011 we were posting record sales, and the system was having a problem with the load. That required all of January to upgrade our servers, licenses, and routers to handle the load. We planned on launching the pay per download "Project Lead" piece of our business in early February, and we came very close to that date, all things considered. It was previously a free download.

We tested the new software and debated exactly how to deploy it. Should we send out a notice or make an announcement? Should we put a free trial ending status remark? The outcome was a hurried rush for deployment with the argument that, even if a single person signed up, it would be additional revenue, and conversely, if anyone complained, what was the difference; it wasn't making any money now, so what was the big deal?

We were bombarded with phone calls and nasty e-mails. I was quite shocked, to be honest. We had been giving the leads away free for over a year, and surely people couldn't expect it to go on forever, right? Wrong! We actually signed up a fair amount of people, but in the end I decided to write a letter to our users explaining the intent and the need for the change, but also that we would lower the price dramatically and give a thirty-day free trial as well.

That move quieted the customer base, and people started signing up at a rate of ten to fifteen per day, but when we looked at the numbers of those who got to the credit card payment page (no charge, just collecting the number), the opt out rate was staggering. We were getting as many as 500 companies per day going through the three-step sign-up process and then 490 of them dropping off.

After running with the logic for over a month, in April we altered the sign-in process based on the information we were collecting, dropping the credit card screen and adding language such as "cancel at any time" and "30-day money back guarantee." Our retention of people signing up for the free trial then improved five or six fold, with fifty or more per day. As the thirty-day trials ended, we began to call and offer a special deal for a one-year membership. That started out well, but it didn't take too long before we realized that we just did not have enough construction content, or project leads, to be able to scale the membership base to numbers that would be significant. We were giving away the invitation to bid software to the general contractors in the hope that they would publish their data to our "Sub Mall," but it appeared we were stalling in bringing on new GCs, resulting in too many subs and not enough content.

26

Another Unique Idea – The Fully Integrated Plan Room

In mid-April I was on the phone with Bart discussing perhaps looking for partners to acquire content to populate the "Sub Mall" with. On that call we decided to reach out to a number of sources for content, including going back to Reed again with a different angle. I would put out calls to four or five companies I knew that might have an interest in licensing or selling us data.

During that conversation Bart revealed that one of our contractors had asked him to go to lunch as a means of thanking him for completing some custom work on their plan room. I asked what the work involved, and he told me they had paid us to wrap their web skins around our technology and that he had bought a URL similar to our customers' so that, when going from page to page, it would appear to his customers that they actually owned the technology because it was incorporated into his website. Bart told me that we probably broke even on the project but picked up a customer, so it was worth it.

Over the course of the next week or so, I did indeed have lengthy discussions with a number of companies to try to make deals to obtain construction leads for resell. But I could see that if we could pull a deal together it wasn't going to be something that would happen overnight and that any deal was going to be complex, costly, and would probably weaken our company or make us overly dependent on the partner.

Bart ended up having that lunch with the customer with the custom website, and he relayed to me that the guy was ecstatic with the look. He shared with Bart that it appeared his subcontractor bid response was much higher than previously as well.

It turned out, that particular contractor used a couple of plan room providers at the same time to take advantage of the various sub communities instead of just one. I asked Bart why the customer felt he was getting a better response. We both thought that he was just proud of his own brand name and was being a bit over the top from a personal standpoint.

However, over the next couple of days, Bart again brought up the supposed phenomenon and suggested maybe we should market it to others. I liked the idea but wondered how many contractors would pay just to make it appear that our software was something they had built into their website. After all, wasn't that just an ego play? Bart reminded me that the customer had insisted that he was getting better results, and I kept asking why. To understand better, I put myself in the position of a sub and walked through the process of what he would encounter during the invitation process of our regular system versus the new one.

It wasn't until I did this same mental exercise with our main competitor's product in mind that it hit me. The competitor was growing rapidly and had a large market share. It was precisely due to the recent success and quick adaptation of the invitation to bid product that had it collapsing under its own weight. The reason being that subs were getting so many invites from various contractors that all looked just like everyone else's. As more and more people used the systems, the notifications, which started to look like junk mail, were being ignored or the general contactor's invite was subconsciously being associated with any contractor using the same third party product. All the invites looked alike, and individual companies did not stand out. Maybe we had something here.

After many hours of discussion, I knew there was only one way to handle the issue properly. We could not afford to be wrong or to execute improperly. I decided to hire an outside firm to do a strategic analysis of the product and of how it would look in the marketplace.

I engaged a firm I had worked with before and moved forward with an immersion study. This is a technique where the marketing company interviewed numerous potential clients to get their feedback on a new product offering. Initial slides and talking points were created and constantly updated based on feedback from each interview so that, at the end of the project, we would be left with a presentation that we could take to market.

After around a dozen interviews with very good feedback, we started to make calls in late July to test the waters. We decided to sell the product for $4,500 per year as opposed to trying to give it away as a means to collect content for the subcontractor project leads. Lo and behold, we sold a couple in August and four in September.

I decided we needed to scale the effort upward. The next four months were consumed with putting together all of the e-mail templates, voice mail scripts, calling process, and talking points to go along with the presentations. In addition, I began interviewing salespeople, hiring three and taking them through the entire training of our company, the industry, and the new product. Toward the end of 2012, I engaged a call center to do the initial calls to set up the appointments for the sales staff. A completely new set of training materials was created, and live one-on-ones were conducted over the holidays for a rollout at the first of the year.

Hiring the staff and the call center was a major gamble, as it would cost just over $100,000 before I would know if it was going to be successful.

In the midst of again shifting gears by switching the focus to the integrated plan room, I received a call from one of our major retail customers. He asked if I would consider expanding our role in the document management efforts we currently provided. He indicated that we had proved ourselves over the last two years and removed his concern about putting all his projects with one company. In addition, the work description would be expanded to include managing the documents earlier and deeper throughout the project. Of course I was thrilled.

In negotiating the pricing and the actual job description, I pointed out to my customer that, in light of the new work added on and considering that my previous life was one of a national retail contractor, would he consider allowing us to actually manage the project as an outsourced construction manager? As I was asking the question, I pushed on with the thought of creating a transparent project management system that could be added to our plan room functionality. He said he would be happy to talk with us about it.

With that in mind and knowing that large corporations paid huge fees to outside firms for project management software, I realized that I would have a distinct advantage if I offered construction management services and could let the owner know that the software was included in my fee, thereby saving him or her money. If I could then prove our software was better than what the owner was currently using, we could sell the entire system regardless of who built the stores.

Another consideration and motivational factor was that I still had the itch to build stores again for quite a few years. I was very good at it, and I sure could use the money, but getting into that business would be the death of my current business, I would be competitive with my own customers. However, being a construction manager or a program manager for a retailer is a different story. I could oversee and manage the GC build process, sell technology, and take on the GCs as potential clients with the leverage of them wanting to work for the retailer I was managing the construction for. Now that could be very exciting.

27

2013 – Serendipity

Beginning the new year, I decided to sell my last collector car to finance the call center and to pursue the new idea of building a project management application. Unfortunately, the car did not meet the low reserve I was willing to sell it for, which put me in a bit of a tight spot.

The title of this chapter is quite appropriate for describing how things came together over about a one-month period straddling the New Year. We were rolling out a new product when we received the call from the retailer asking for expanded services. That triggered the thought of doing construction management, which required additional software to do correctly. That thought process tied in with what would be needed a year from now when current subscribers for our new integrated product were up for renewals. We could expand the plan room to include some project management tools and use those same tools to do the program management for retailers.

What if we were to create an additional company to build the program/project management software and sales and brought in an investor? I have already stated how I feel about investor money, but I learned a lot from the experience, and it would be a separate company with a structured deal allowing Pantera to use a stripped-down version of the software created to enhance the plan room. We would then have a significantly expanded offering for general contractors with the Pantera product and own a portion of a company that would sell the full product to owner groups. That product would go beyond just project management and include design, budget, and forecast modules that would not be part of the Pantera product.

I spent the second weekend in January putting together the talking points for the new opportunity so I could share it with a couple of people who might have a strategic interest in being partnered with the new company, tentatively called 3PM. I created a twelve-page PowerPoint presentation to outline the idea and shared it with a very large architectural firm that I knew did a lot of program management, and I shared it with a friend who expressed interest in the idea.

The meeting with the architects went very well. They stated that, if I could indeed build a product that would do what I had just laid out, I would be a very rich man and they would be interested. The presentation to my friend ended with an offer to be a partner in Pantera as a whole without the separate entities.

Two to three weeks went by with no word from the architects. I decided to move forward with the offer from the friend. Sitting down to negotiate, however, proved to be discouraging, the amount of money he was willing to put up dropped from one million to three hundred thousand dollars. I left the meeting knowing there was no way we could build the technology for that amount.

I decided to move forward anyway with the promise that we would add features that would certainly enhance our offering.

While waiting to work out the formal proposal and the terms and conditions for my friend to invest, I decided to explore the possibility of licensing the software or partnering with another company to have a more robust offering rather than trying to build the software from scratch. I had a list of twelve high level project management companies that were in the cloud based project management space, and only one of them was actually in the construction sector. My pitch to those companies was to allow us to integrate with their product, adding our preconstruction tools and then modifying their system to comply with construction practices.

Out of the top twenty project management systems in existence, none of them resided in the construction space. The other construction specific project management software products that were on the market were written from the developer's perspective, or that of an architect who centers his or her thinking around the documents, or a leasing company with emphasis on the deal, or a contractor with strong scheduling but who is weak somewhere else. None of the construction specific software had any regard for PMI compliance, which is a standard used in conjunction with PMBOK (*Project Management Book of Knowledge*). This standard is used by all of the sophisticated project management products and is used in a number of other industries such as manufacturing, aerospace, IT development, and the rest. It was my feeling that, if I could convince one of those high-level companies to partner with us, we would have a product far superior to any in the space. I also noticed that numerous Project Management firms were consolidating or being funded by Venture Capital firms.

Evil in the Boardroom

While I was able to enter into preliminary negotiations with a few companies, there was only one company that saw the value of what we were doing and could fill our needs, their name was Project Insight. The trick was to negotiate a deal whereby we could get an exclusive for the construction space without breaking the bank and be able to add in the other terms that would protect us in the event of a sale by either entity. Many other terms were still flying back and forth when I received a call from my friend who was going to invest. He was backing out. His company had decided the timing was not good due to the unknowns with the cost of the new national health care act and the uncertainty of the next year.

I continued negotiations with Project Insight. I knew that, if I could get the deal I was working on, we could get the money to move forward from somewhere.

Of course, having the best product on the market that no one had ever heard of was not a great story either. So I started to put together a plan to raise money for a sales force when, out of the blue, my old friend and former VP from Plan Express called to let me know that the Y factor was selling off PEI and it was being acquired by NRI, a large reprographer out of New York. Bart suggested the idea of approaching them with the thought of investing in our product. It would supplement their product and give us feet on the street. It would also help them get back into the technology space they had all but lost. I reached out to them through my contact who was now running Plan Express and arranged a meeting in New York to lay out my idea.

Within a two-week period, I was to attend a trade show in Dallas, travel to New York to pitch the idea, finish the negotiation with

Project Insight, and sign the deal, which required a good deal of money we did not have. I pushed forward.

While in Dallas I spoke with my friend. He said he was sorry about backing out of the deal but that the $300,000 was just too much and maybe his company could look at it again in six months. I let him know that I could probably get it done with $200,000, and instead of a year of development to build from scratch and the uncertainty of a complete product, we could launch a game changer within six months due to the deal I was close to pulling together. I asked if he would consider a loan that he could later convert to stock if he wished. He asked me to write it up and send it to him.

Within days, I finalized the deal points with Project Insight and headed to New York. At this point, I had no financing and no real knowledge as to whether the software could be configured to beat the existing products in construction. I did not want to meet with NRI and claim that I had a product that would be a game changer without proof. So I hired a consultant to do a gap analysis of the feature set of a combined Pantera/Project Insight offering against the popular construction software product ProCore and the legacy (and recently sold for $47 million) product Constructware.

I arrived in New York at 9:00 p.m. on a Monday with my meeting scheduled for 9:00 a.m. the next morning with NRI. I received a call at 10:00 p.m. with the results of the first comparison from my consultant, who said that our product would indeed be superior to ProCore. It wasn't until two days later that I was told that the product would be vastly superior to Constructware. That being said, I went to the meeting without a signed deal with Project

Evil in the Boardroom

Insight, although all terms were agreed on. I did not have the money to sign the deal, however.

My pitch to NRI was simple: invest in Pantera and sell our product to its customer base. NRI would be selling a product it currently did not have that would be better than any other on the market. The commission would be similar to other products NRI sold, but the company would own a piece of the product. I also asked that NRI help bring in another large player so that the impact would be national. The meeting seemed to go well, and the CEO asked for a demonstration of the product the week after. I could not say who the project management company was yet for obvious reasons.

Upon my arrival back at our home office, I received word from my friend via a text message that said, "We are in" (for the financing). I immediately drafted a loan document that was returned signed the next day, which was fortunate, Project Insight was in town and wanted to meet and sign our agreement the day after, which we did. Whew!

The process for integrating Project Insight into the Pantera platform was no small chore. We began with finalizing all the contracts and tightening the exclusivity and sale provisions to make the deal bankable. We had a team fly to California for training, and I led the process of mapping out how the two systems would work together with the help of the PI team. The next five to six months would be dedicated to coding and tying the systems together. We would be able to sell to a much larger audience with an end-to-end product unlike anything in the industry. It was preconstruction and project management on one platform in the cloud.

28

And the next Story Begins

As I write this, 2013 is wrapping up and we are heading into 2014 well positioned with our new preconstruction and project management system; Pantera Project Insight.

We have booked several trade shows, hired two more salespeople with more on the way, and the company continues to operate in the black (although no one is rich yet).

The temptation to do another venture capital deal is still out there. Do we stay small and perhaps miss an opportunity to be the market leader? The next six months will tell the story, and if I do decide to go the VC route, I will be a little older and a whole lot wiser (and perhaps have content for a second book).

My hope is that, after you have finished reading this, you will take a bit of the information it contains to heart for practical use. The status of Pantera should be easy to obtain by checking the site. www.panteratools.com. Remember, if you're considering a venture capital deal, call me first, maybe I can help.

THE END...for now.

Update on Pantera

I had ended my writings at the beginning of 2014 and was waiting on editing and final design and frankly just not in a rush to finish the book. It is now late May and it appears that we are getting close to sending the book to print so I will add this update to be as current as possible.

Training sales people seems to be the biggest obstacle right now. Trying to expand the business solely on excess cash flow is a slow process. The learning curve is a bit steep and we are putting a curriculum in place to minimize this curve for new employees but it is an agonizingly slow process. We have developed the metrics to prove that for every dollar we invest in sales we grow our top line revenue by 3 to 4 times but it takes months to generate that first return assuming the sales person works out.

To overcome this problem and jumpstart the process I was convinced by an old friend to take some additional "friendly" money from someone I know rather than wait out the earning your way method. He asked if he could invest in a 500,000 dollar round at a fair valuation because he was seriously interested in the company and liked what he saw. I agreed and went ahead and had an attorney draft the agreement only to have the friend decide not to do the investment as other priorities took precedent. A total waste of time and money..

Meanwhile we won the 2014 Constructech Top Product Award for Bid Management! This resulted in numerous calls from Venture Capital firms wanting to learn more. There is much to be excited about and they share that excitement but everyone who has called has criteria that requires at least 5 million in revenue for them to make an investment. As we now are in the 2 million dollar per year sales range we are far short of meeting that requirement. The truth is that when we get to the 3 million dollar range, at least 50 to 60% of that extra million will be profit thereby negating the need for an investment, so we are operating in a bit of a Catch 22 zone.

We have also received calls from two very large firms who have expressed interest in buying our company outright. The first of these seemed to be quite serious and it resulted in 3 meetings and a face to face in our Wisconsin office where things felt like they were progressing rapidly only to fall out about a week before their 1st quarter earnings release. The stock has dropped 50% in 1 month! I guess they have other things to figure out rather than acquiring us. The other company called a week ago and said they still have an interest in us as a means to fill a hole in their product offering but they are looking at a couple of companies so we will have to wait and see.

Three nights ago we received notification that Pantera was going to be announced as one of the TOP 50 technology companies in construction by Constructech's editorial board. That will probably get the phones ringing as well.

For current updates see our website at www.panteratools.com

Jack's résumé on LinkedIn:

(referenced from page 117)

- Backed by two of the Southeast's top venture capital firms, is the construction industry's leading online document management technology company serving over 1,000 of the nation's largest general contractors and retailers, including GAP, Starbucks, Tiffany, Wal-Mart, AutoZone, and Lowes.

- Hired to replace company founder as CEO and develop and execute a strategy to engineer a complete business turnaround and business model change from outsourced print provider to web-based, asset-light, variable-cost technology business.

- Developed and implemented entirely new go-to-market and pricing strategy to reflect the massive shift from paper to digital distribution of construction documentation.

- Increased gross margins from <30% to >50% in under 12 months by shedding nationwide network of company-owned print facilities and outsourcing print fulfillment to network of private label print providers and changing focus/strategy of company to technology and digital content management and distribution.

- Eliminated over $500K in monthly expenses while retaining and developing top company talent.

- Engineered highly successful sale of the company to largest competitor for a combination of cash and preferred stock despite worst economic conditions for the AEC industry in decades.

Collen Realty's professional staff; Valerie McNamara (seated), from left to right; Bill Jensen, Realtor, Nancy Pierce, Realtor, Dewayne Adamson, Realtor, Carla Krueger, Realtor and Colleen Deininger, Broker.

A very young Real Estate Broker

Lakeshore Mechanical – 1983

State Construction – 1988

Alert Service, State Permit, 1993

Every little thing a biker could want

By Ann Piccininni
SPECIAL TO THE TRIBUNE

Call of the Wild
325 W. Town Line Road, Mundelein
Hours: 10 a.m. to 7 p.m. Monday through Friday, 9 a.m. to 5 p.m. Saturday, and 10 a.m. to 2 p.m. Sunday.
Phone: 708-970-9453

DeWayne Adamson was a retail contractor facing career "burn-out." When he asked his contracting partner to buy out his end of the business, Adamson decided to start a new one reflecting his boyhood love for growling, two-wheeled vehicles.

Thus, Call of the Wild was born. The shop features all manner of motorcycle accessories, from leather to chrome, and a few motorcycles, too.

"I started doing a little research, and I thought maybe I could build motorcycles and sell them," the Bristol, Wis., resident said.

The store, open since mid-November, features Adamson's own Ellis motorcycles. "I would compare it to a Harley-Davidson Softail," he said.

The Ellis model in the showroom is priced at $23,000, a figure that tops most Harleys, Adamson said, but includes some extras, like mag wheels and a special paint job.

There are also several used Harley motorcycles on display and a brand-new Illusion, a bike recently introduced by a California manufacturer, Adamson said.

The accessories are highlighted by the store's decor, dominated by a giant Harley dashboard suspended from the ceiling. There are manhole covers inlaid in the floor. And all around are the familiar vestiges of biker culture: leather jackets, helmets, boots. There are motorcycle parts, including mirrors, lights, belt guards, cylinder covers and axle caps.

In the gift section, Adamson said, shoppers can check out the Harley-licensed watches, belts, biker wallets.

The store's clothing line includes bomber jackets, vests, T-shirts, sweatshirts, scarves, hats, gloves, bandannas and baseball caps. Some of the clothes bear the store's logo, an eagle grasping the letters of the store's name in its talons.

Adamson also offers motorcycle owners a service department, where a certified technician is available for repairs and maintenance.

Tribune photo by Stan Policht
DeWayne Adamson stocks his Mundelein shop, Call of the Wild, with all manner of motorcycle accessories.

Call of the Wild - In the store 1994

First Chopper with Digital Mirror 1994

177

First Trade show for Call of the Wild – 1994

Plan Express pic from PEI

Plan Express

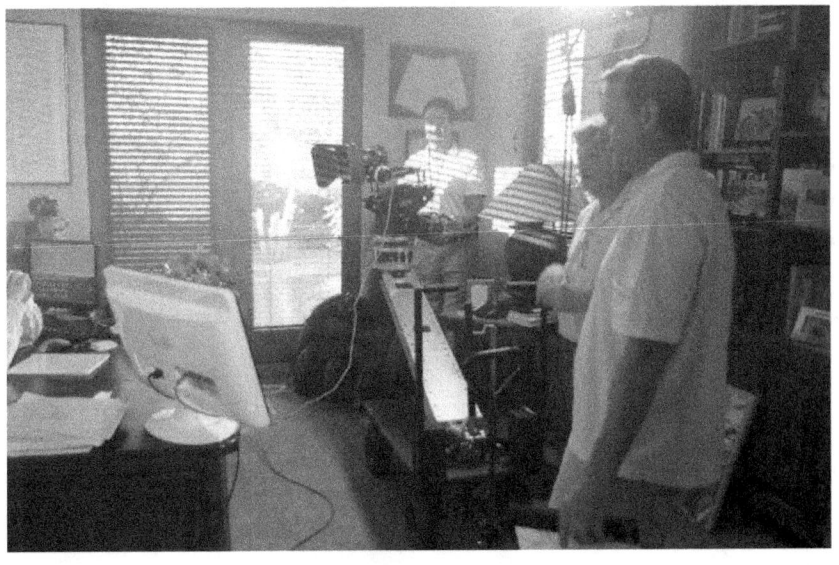

Making a movie 2009

Hence the name!   Pantera

Pantera's debut

Pantera's first Trade Show – 2013

DeWayne's unique background encompasses numerous aspects of the Construction and Technology sectors.

His expertise in Construction began as a skilled tradesman. At an early age he was quickly promoted through the ranks to become a Project Manager/Estimator and then a Vice President of a prominent Mechanical Contractor. Gaining knowledge from one of Chicago's largest Mechanical Contractors, Dewayne ran numerous Major construction projects in the downtown area. In 1986 a local General Contractor offered Dewayne an opportunity as a Sr. Project Manager in the General Construction arena. Specializing in Retail Construction, Dewayne ran over 700 projects. In 1992 Dewayne founded the first National Permit Expediting firm, a National Maintenance Company, and Co-founded one of the Largest Retail Construction firms in the country. All of these companies were successfully sold. He went on to create a motorcycle manufacturing facility with a high end boutique as well as a full motorcycle service center and machine shop. In 1993 he co-founded Plan Express, a national printing and distribution company. In 1999 Dewayne became the sole owner of Plan Express and went on a mission to make PEI the first Online Planroom with Print functionality. This technology was launched successfully and PEI grew to one of the largest print and logistics companies in the world, introducing many new technology products along the way. The story of PEI is one of drama and intrigue and delves into the pitfalls of bringing in an outside investor. Following the turmoil of PEI came the birth of Adamson's current start up, Pantera Global Technology.

Startups referenced in this book include:

Lakeshore Mechanical

Expicon / State Permit

Inscriptions

Alert Retail Service

Lakeview Construction

Plan Express

Call of the Wild

Ellis Motorcycle

Pantera Global Technology

Panteratools

Pantera Project Insight

To contact the Author visit www.DewayneAdamson.com

2012 victory/ the book/ my testimony

www.ingramcontent.com/pod-product-compliance
Lightning Source LLC
Chambersburg PA
CBHW051649170526
45167CB00001B/398